Blurbs for: *Beyond Autism*

"*Beyond Autism* is the closest that anyone has come to entering the mind, unlocking the medical challenges, exploring traditional and non-traditional therapies, and grasping the potential of an autistic child. **Unparalleled in its honesty, compassion and unconditional love.** A must read for physicians, parents, and researchers who want to understand autism."
—Sheldon Krimsky, Lenore Stern Professor
of Humanities and Social Sciences Tufts University

"Helena takes us on **a journey of transformation with heart and honesty,** applicable not only the challenges of autism, but to the trial's life hands us all."
—Ken Siri, author of
Cutting-Edge Therapies for Autism

"**Hjalmarsson reminds us that even in the most trying of circumstances, there is always light, a lesson, and above all, love—if we allow ourselves the space and permission to experience them.** *Beyond Autism* is a testament to the power of the human spirit and the never-ending quest to connect with our children."
—Julie Obradovic, author of *An Unfortunate Coincidence:*
A Mother's Life inside the Autism Controversy

"Helena Hjalmarsson gives us a genuine view into life a shared with a child afflicted with autism – the pain and frustration but also the joy and mystery of walking a spiritual path with a genuine, loving person. *Beyond Autism* **is fearless and honest. Hjalmarsson tells autism like it is, courageously.**"
—Louis Conte, author of *Vaccine Injuries:*
Documented Adverse Reactions to Vaccines

"***Beyond Autism* divulges epiphanies as gifts only seen through a special needs parent's lens.** Helena reminds us to reclaim our self-compassion and *Beyond Autism* ultimately defines the autism paradox."
—Lori Ashley Taylor, author of *Dragonfly:*
A Daughter's Emergence From Autism . . .
A Practical Guide for Parents

"It's easy to lose sight of what is truly important, especially if it's been staring you in the face all along. *Beyond Autism* **is about appreciating the wonder, beauty and creativity** all our children on the autism spectrum bring us each and every day, regardless how it may appear."

—Karen Simmons, Founder, CEO Autism Today, Autismtoday.com, author of *The Official Autism 101 Manual*

"In *Beyond Autism*, **Helena Hjalmarsson lays bare with raw honesty both the extreme challenges and the moments of exquisite beauty in raising a child severely affected by autism.** She speaks openly about moments of awe-inspiring anguish and pain in a way that many parents experience but cannot express, [while] her love and respect for Lina shine throughout this memoir."

—Kim Mack Rosenberg, author of *The Parent's Autism Sourcebook*

"If you want to understand what it feels like to raise a child with severe autism, *Beyond Autism* is an excellent place to start. Helena Hjalmarsson's memoir about her life with daughter Lina reveals the heartaches, joys and spiritual gifts of this parenting journey. **Written in clear prose, the memoir is filled with beauty, trauma, and grace.**"

—Mary Holland, faculty, NYU School of Law

"*Beyond Autism* is a treasure of immense honesty and faith, a tribute to the joyful chaos of pursuit . . . of medical answers, philosophical understanding, spiritual awakening, and the ironic **reminder that it is sometimes the unknowing that keeps us most present and self aware.**"

—Amanda Friedman, MSEd, SBL, Executive Director Atlas Foundation for Autism

"This book **truly took me beyond my understanding of the physical and emotional circumstances of autism** by painting pictures from the vivid palate of Lina's colorful world instead of my own."

—Del Bigtree, Producer of *Vaxxed*

Beyond Autism

MY LIFE WITH LINA

Helena Hjalmarsson, M.A., L.C.S.W., L.P.

Skyhorse Publishing

Skyhorse Publishing books may be purchased in bulk at special discounts for sales promotion, corporate gifts, fund-raising, or educational purposes. Special editions can also be created to specifications. For details, contact the Special Sales Department, Skyhorse Publishing, 307 West 36th Street, 11th Floor, New York, NY 10018 or info@skyhorsepublishing.com.

Skyhorse® and Skyhorse Publishing® are registered trademarks of Skyhorse Publishing, Inc.®, a Delaware corporation.

Visit our website at www.skyhorsepublishing.com.

10 9 8 7 6 5 4 3 2 1

Library of Congress Cataloging-in-Publication Data is available on file.

Cover design by Brian Peterson
Cover photograph by Helena Hjalmarsson

Print ISBN: 978-1-5107-4625-1
Ebook ISBN: 978-1-5107-4626-8

Printed in the United States of America

To Lina and Elsa and my three best friends,
Gabriella, Tony, and Agnes.

Thank you for being here with me. I love you.

And to my editor, Lilly Golden, whose kindness, intelligence, and
charm makes me want to write another book.

"The wound is the place where the Light enters you."

—Rumi

Contents

Foreword

by Dick Russell

It's undeniable that the rise in diagnosis of children with autism or related disabilities is alarming, if not epidemic. The latest figures of the Centers for Disease Control released in April 2018 list one in every 59 American kids now considered autistic. In 2007, it was one out of 150. In the 1980s, it was one out of 2,000.

This means that more than two million U.S. families today experience the overwhelming challenge of raising such a special needs child. For many, "coping" or "managing" are words that fail to compute. What to do amid a constantly-changing reality with no apparent solution often makes life for parents and siblings almost unbearably difficult.

That is why this painfully honest and deeply moving book is so important. A psychoanalyst with a master's degree in child development, Helena Hjalmarsson first came forward with a wrenching personal account in a 2013 memoir, *Finding Lina*. In *Beyond Autism*, her now-teenaged daughter's story explores alternative avenues of healing that bring to the forefront Lina's unique gifts.

Not that the book paints a rosy picture. Mother and daughter go through agonizing confrontations and even a near-death experience together. There are days and nights of not only uncertainty but hopelessness. There is trial-and-error in the author's painstaking efforts to find the proper diet, the right caregivers, the most helpful practices outside the standard medical model. The reader will accompany the family to encounters with an African shaman and a Navajo healer, both of whose insights prove invaluable, and to discover various techniques of Neuro-Movement and RPM (Rapid Prompting Method) to stimulate Lina's latent abilities.

As a father who has faced similar situations with my now-grown son, once diagnosed with schizophrenia but exhibiting many characteristics on the autism spectrum, I find much to relate to here. Yes, the sudden unexplainable mood swings, but also the uncanny response to the invisible energy of a person or in a room, the non-linear sense of time, the ability to see and feel things beyond the ken of "ordinary" humans like ourselves. Seeing colors, sensing frequencies, tuning in to undisclosed thoughts and feelings in another person: rational Westerners label this "otherworldly" and strange, while indigenous cultures extol and celebrate these as gifts of the gods.

So in many ways, Lina becomes her mother's teacher—about learning to be in the moment, about the importance of remaining open to the unconventional, about the paradox that life is, about compassion, and ultimately about love. Through it all, a witnessing that Lina's differences are not so much a curse as a blessing—to her mother and father, her younger sister, and the larger tribe that gathers in the ongoing search for healing and peace.

Lina remains up against very serious challenges. Yet despite her sometimes frenzied and incomprehensible actions, she often has a calming effect on others. She finds her solace in the vast ocean, and displays a remarkable courage in battling not only mental confusion but physical ailments that seem to come with the territory. In the process of going beyond the spectrum with Lina, her mother too finds courage and solace. That should serve as the primary lesson of this heartfelt memoir, not only for parents facing similar hardships but for all of us seeking to become more empathic human beings.

DICK RUSSELL is the author of *My Mysterious Son: A Life-Changing Passage Between Schizophrenia and Shamanism.*

INTRODUCTION

This is my second attempt to describe life with my daughter Lina. She is now fifteen years old. After my first book about Lina in 2013, I had planned to write another book, this time about Lina's little sister, Elsa. Throughout the years with Lina, the challenges and triumphs, the lessons that come from having a child who, at 3 1/2, suddenly regressed into the incomprehensible abyss of autism, I have wondered what the autism experience was like for Elsa, who is two years younger than Lina. There is a sweetness, an uncompromising compassion that I see in Elsa, that so often seems to be present in individuals who have been standing by, watching their brothers and sisters suffer in ways that the world around them can little understand. We are too busy being puzzled by autism itself to focus on what it is like to stand by, as a sibling, watching your sister's or brother's struggle. And the irony is that, besides the children who have this condition, no one understands it as well as their siblings. Whether they like it or not, they are the true experts on autism.

What is it like to have a sister or brother who can turn a crowded supermarket into an eerie freeze in a matter of seconds? How does it affect the siblings of children with autism to see the police question their parents about their sister's or brother's deafening screaming, headbanging, biting, kicking, or latest running away down a busy city street? What is it like for the siblings to over and over again be left on their own with their sadness and fear as they watch their parent desperately try to prevent their sister or brother from turning their house into firewood? How does it feel to hear your parents fill up your whole world with obsessive, incessant talk about the next alternative treatment for your sibling? What is it like to know that you have more privilege, more well-being, more opportunity, more responsibility, more expectations, more autonomy, more luck, more obligation, more friends, better grades, and more enthusiastic teachers than your sister or brother with autism?

I wanted to write the untold story of Elsa, Lina's younger sister. And I didn't just want to write it to benefit someone who is a sibling to a person with autism, or for the parent of an autistic child with siblings, who may have recognized, somewhere along the arduous line of trying to keep it all together, that they know less than they thought about their other child's experience. I was, in fact, mostly hoping that writing about Elsa would help *me* understand her quiet experience as she observed her sister struggle through years of sensory mayhem, uncontrollable tantrums, loss of words, and oceans of confusion, sorrow, panic, and disintegration.

I was going to write this story because the storm had settled. Lina, at the time, was doing so much better. We were all sitting around a big metaphorical fireplace, licking our wounds from the battle. It was quiet. Peaceful. Elsa's bright, clear voice broke the silence. Finally, I had a chance to listen to Elsa's story, reclaim the space that had shrunk right in front of her one-and-a-half-year-old eyes as her older sister transformed from a charming, loving, verbally skilled big sister to a person who turned Elsa's life into an incomprehensible tornado. I wanted to re-create Elsa's space. Because her life is just as important, just as urgent, just as relevant as her beautiful older sister's.

However, five pages into this new book, I asked Elsa, is it ok if I write about you? And do you know what she said? She said, "No."

She'd already found her space. She didn't need me to give it back to her. She is so much more than a sibling to a sister with autism. She doesn't need to define herself in that way. She sees herself. She knows herself. And she will express herself in whatever way she wants, in her own time, with her own words. Consequently, there is no book about Elsa. But somehow, miraculously, there is a little sister who knows how to claim and protect her own space.

So instead of writing about Elsa, I began the writing of *Beyond Autism*. But this book, like the first one, *Finding Lina*, is really more about finding myself, my own internal resources, my own inner vision, my own peace and joy, and my own ability to be compassionate with myself. Because without it, I'm nothing. A more honest title might be *Finding Helena 2*. Because the more I get to know Lina, the more time and the more experiences we have together, the less clear it becomes who we are finding in our journey together, Lina and I.

Autism is the biggest contradiction I have ever come across in my life, one of the most thoroughly misunderstood conditions on the planet. Lina is one of the most complete human beings I have ever met. I prefer her company to most others. She is egoless, genuine, and unreserved in the way she loves her fellow human beings. And yet, the suffering that she has endured since the age of three and a half, when she had her second MMR (measles, mumps, and rubella) vaccine and immediately afterward had her first of innumerable seizures and lost everything, including her speech, takes more than one book to describe. Why would I try? I want to be very clear. It's because along this journey, in the middle of this almost unendurable challenge, I have found so much beauty in

Lina as well as in life in general that you will never hear me say that I regret having Lina. Every parent of a child with autism has their own way of figuring out how to keep their head above water. Lina has shown me that regretting our situation or our life together would be like depriving myself of all the possibility that sometimes only shows up when you're banging on the door of the impossible.

However, I also think it would be a mistake to try to deny the fact that—with the exception of a small percentage of people on the spectrum who are fully functional and contributing members of society, able to express themselves, feed themselves, hold down a job or even a relationship (which is quite a challenge even for ordinary people of this era)—life with autism is very often brutal, bordering on the absurd.

Autism, for most families with one or more children affected by this compilation of severe challenges, has very little to do with ordinary life the way most of us understand it. It's pain and discomfort, leaky gut, yeast, urinary tract infections, PANDAS, PANS, extreme diet, sensory avoidance, sensory craving, proprioceptive disorientation, autoimmune disorders, candida, viral infections, brain inflammation. It's seizures and all the many, often violent, self-destructive, out-of-control manifestations of such breakdowns of the brain. It's bruised arms, bite marks, fat lips, headaches from hard, adrenaline-driven jabs, broken glass, broken furniture, broken dreams, ripped books, endless screaming, lives torn up in a thousand pieces. It's incontinence that can last long into the teenage years, sometimes for a lifetime. It's separation, divorce, alienation, loneliness. It's depression, confusion and disorganization, disorientation and memory loss from lack of sleep. It's loss of career, loss of romantic life, loss of friends, loss of dignity and hope. It's living on a different planet and lacking the words to describe to the noninitiated what this planet is like. It's the unspeakable, the indescribable, the unlivable. It's relentless, agitated OCD and weeks and months of relapse, just when you thought you had found what works.

My books are primarily for the parents, siblings, and caretakers of children with autism.

They are two of an increasing number of "you are not alone" literary statements from parents of children with autism to the people whose lives often get in the way of a relationship with a larger community. I want them to be like a meeting place. A smile of recognition. A reason for a little dark joke among parents. The beginning of a friendship between my child and yours, real or imaginary. The beginning of a partnership between parents struggling in incomprehensible spaces.

I am hoping that it's also somehow a door toward something better. Something as egoless as our beautiful and mysterious children. Something as spacious and free as the place only those who suffer immensely choose to go to while still on this Earth. Because whenever Lina is not in mayhem, she is in heaven. Whenever she is not having a hard time, she seems so free of the burdens of a past and a future, so deeply present and accepting of the moment, so genuinely thrilled with and embracing of her life just as it is. Whether she is taking that particular breath, eating that particular piece of cauliflower, or listening to that particular Bob Dylan song . . . whenever she is not suffering, it seems to me that she is at that enlightened, awakened place that most people struggle for a whole lifetime just to catch a glimpse of.

A friend of mine, a pretty tough policeman and the father of three boys on the spectrum, once said to me, as if it were the most obvious thing in the world, "Well of course you want a teacher that's aware of spiritual reality! Our children are spiritual beings." This is Lina's gift to me and to anyone who spends time with her. Maybe because of her suffering, maybe because of her calling, or maybe because of something else that I cannot explain, Lina is connected with so many frequencies other than ours. She is connected to other spaces and places and mysteries much more intriguing, colorful, and beautiful than ours. I sometimes get the feeling that she is running out of reasons to spend much conscious time in our frequency. Most of us are disconnected. We have so little perspective. We are often so enslaved by what we can see and hear, taste, and touch. So trapped by our expectations of how we think things should be. So untrained in going beyond, seeing the invisible, sensing the divine. Not Lina.

And as I try to follow Lina along, catch a glimpse of her rich inner world, understand how her joy can be so complete in spite of everything she has been through, I learn what I need to do, too. I have to learn to live unconditionally. I have to learn how to squeeze every ounce of joy out of every possible situation, laugh with my whole heart, welcome everything, move on quickly, and drop my entangled thought process continuously. Pack light. Joy is always here. Peace is always here. Life is a dream. What's real and true is always complete, never compromised or beaten down, no matter what happens to us.

I have been blessed with circumstances that give me the biggest incentive to reach beyond my own personal identity and experience, to find inside of me, connected to all that is, that which isn't personal, or temporary, but complete, whole, and happy. When my life is so full of challenge that it seems almost unbelievable, I find what Lina has known all along, the real, true, and free beyond my own beliefs. I find that this life, in fact, is unbelievable. Nothing to take too seriously. Nothing to obsess about or trying to manipulate. And I try to stay here. But even when I dip back into my life and my identity, my feelings and experiences and beliefs, I know that the truth, the freedom that Lina so easily tunes into, is always there, whether I recognize it or not. It's always there, not just for Lina, not just for me, but for everyone.

CHAPTER ONE

PANDAS and Acute Mycoplasma Infection

L INA AND I are standing in shallow ocean water, our feet touching the sand. It is a red flag day. The waves are not as high as yesterday, but the water got murky and brown overnight. We are in Fire Island, New York, for an extended week in August, after cancelling our trip to Sweden.

We had planned this trip for a long time. Tony, my ex-husband and the father of Lina and Elsa, was going to come, too. The family trip to Sweden was inspired by the West African shaman Malidoma, who met Lina, Tony, and me and did divinations and ancestral readings for all three of us. One of the outcomes was seeing the importance of taking Lina to Sweden, where she would be able to communicate in her mother tongue and be in the space of her ancestors. Lina's first language was Swedish, before she lost all her language and ability to play and developed acute sensory processing issues.

Diet, homeotoxicology, biomedical interventions, floor time, Son-Rise, Sound Therapy, NeuroMovement, love, and ongoing and intense working with Lina one-on-one on every level helped my daughter tremendously. But since of end of May of 2016, right before Lina's thirteenth birthday, she experienced a dramatic setback, with acute OCD, violent outbursts, and mental and physical agitation and turmoil. After a year of increasing bliss and lots of new developments in Lina's language, interactivity, and general comfort level, Lina's struggles had suddenly intensified. In the last few months, they had reached a new and intimidating crescendo, right around the time we were to hop on our eight-hour flight to Denmark and drive to the summer house by the coast in southern Sweden that one of my brothers and I inherited after our parents' deaths. With Lina's frequently occurring breakdowns, it didn't seem wise or safe to put Lina and Elsa in any kind of complicated or confined situation, so we found a last-minute rental in Seaview, Fire Island, instead.

The ocean has always been Lina's friend, before and after her regression into autism. She has always known how to interact even with very powerful waves and is a strong, however unconventional, swimmer. She does a mean dog-paddle. Whenever she is in the water, she goes to her own higher ground, talking, singing, and finding the kind of peace so hard to come by in her everyday life.

This was a day of stormy waters, no different from many such days. Our wonderful old babysitter, I'll call her Erika, who had recently gotten married and moved out of New York City, still worked with us now and then, whenever she had a break in her regular schedule. She was standing on shore watching, ready to help out, should we need an extra hand. In light of Lina's recent difficulties—which looked like they may be caused by something called PANDAS (Pediatric Autoimmune Neuropsychiatric Disorders Associated with Streptococcus), a group of autoimmune disorders with very severe consequences—I had decided that we would always have two people at the beach with Lina, especially in or near the ocean.

Lina and I just stood at the water's edge, watching the surf roll in toward us, feeling the energy of the waves as they broke and streamed over our legs up to our waists. To me, the ocean is always beautiful. Always interesting. I too feel so connected with myself and everything around me when I'm near it. And even during these very hard times, when Lina's feet touched the water, her OCD subsided.

I've gone over what happened next a thousand times. Suddenly Lina and I were just swept out by the current. We were quietly and quickly removed from the shore and pulled farther and farther out. Lina started deliberately swimming back toward shore. I tried to signal to Erika for help, but she froze; there wasn't much she could have done at that point. There weren't many people on the beach that day, and no lifeguard in sight. Lina started to whimper as she realized what was happening. I tried to swim her to shore by holding her in front of me and doing a one-armed backstroke, but she wouldn't have it. I had to put one of my arms around her upper back and paddle with my other arm, kicking my legs, but the shore just seemed farther and farther away. Lina became visibly afraid and kept pulling me under. I couldn't breathe. I tried to scream, but no sounds came out of my throat. I have never felt the power of the ocean in this way, and I felt totally helpless. I have never felt fear in the way I felt it out there.

I don't think it was me who saved us, but at some point, somehow, I felt the ground again under my feet. Whatever strength I had left vanished. I couldn't move myself or Lina another inch forward. A woman in the shallow water not far from us came over to help and dragged me and Lina in toward the sandy beach. Lina and I lay in the warm sand for a long time, not saying anything. Erika sat next to us, also not saying anything. It was shocking for her to see Lina in this condition, since the last time Erika had worked with her, she had been doing so much better. In the middle of everything, I had somehow blanked out on preparing Erika for what Lina was going through before she showed up at Fire Island. And while Erika had always been exceptionally balanced, competent, and unafraid of challenges in her work with Lina, I still believe this week was at least as traumatic for her as it was for the rest of us.

The rest of that day Lina was in good form, laughing, calm, comfortable, happy, and with very little obsessive talk. We spent the evening wandering around the little roads on Fire Island, looking for the "yellow deer" that she was so intrigued by. Perhaps she was really fascinated that the deer freely and confidently roam Fire Island, living side by side with islanders and summer guests, oblivious to the dangers of cars, which are not allowed here. Or maybe Lina was talking about the deer medicine from the Native American shamanic tradition where different animals, referred to as power-animals, are understood to offer humans protection, strength, insight, and guidance. Lina only sometimes finds the words to talk to me about this, but I believe that for her, when an animal comes to her in her dreams or when she is awake, she listens and feels protected by their particular power. With love, compassion and gentleness, and unwavering determination, Deer Medicine melts away even the most monstrous challenge. The deer as a medicine animal can teach us to touch others and ourselves with unconditional kindness, without trying to force anyone to change but simply to love ourselves and others just as we are. The deer teaches us that fear does not live in the same place as gentleness and love. To me, Lina's ongoing talk about the yellow deer served as instruction. It was her way of letting me know how to most effectively help her through her challenges.

Eventually, "yellow deer" turned into "yellow tiger." After our near-drowning experience, Lina referred to "the yellow tiger in the ocean." Interestingly, the yellow tiger, in Chinese shaman tradition, is the king of all tigers and provides great strength and protection in times of overpowering adversity.

To me, our experience of almost being swept out for good in that dark, murky water had great metaphoric significance. Our existence during the preceding months had felt like a nightmare. Often, I asked myself how I would get through the next day, the next hour, the next meal. It had begun around the end of May, when Lina suddenly got stuck on certain ideas. I remember the night where all she could say was "red and black, red and black, red and black . . ." We were lying in my bedroom late at night; she was too anxious to be by herself. Her OCD was relentless. It was past midnight, and Lina was foaming at her mouth, repeating "red and black red and black" in a never-ending anxious stream. I felt like we both were in prison. I went with her, saying, "red and black," quickly like her, then a little slower, with a little pause in between, introducing variation to allow her brain a moment's rest, to allow her brain to perceive something in between the words. She approved and kept on another twenty minutes chanting a little slower, "red and black." I said, "Lina, how do you feel about green?" She ignored me and then said, "Red and black red and black red and black, red ... and ... black ... Green."

I tried to contain the sense of ecstasy I felt over this color variation. Green in that moment seemed like finding the road back home, our path from OCD hell toward heaven. A heaven where everything would be flowing again. Where Lina's brain would be receptive to outside impressions, where ideas would flow, and where sometimes there was no grasping, no wanting what she can't have, no miserable attachment, just being. Very soon, though, green was integrated, captivated, taken hostage by OCD and became the new red and black. The night continued, with us chanting away together. If Lina was going to be in OCD land, I would at least not leave her there alone. We would be there for as long as we had to be there, and when she was done, I would be done, too. At some point in the early morning, Lina fell asleep, exhausted. She looked so peaceful in her sleep—her face so soft, her hands open, her breathing so calm and full. It was hard to believe that she had been clenching her fists, throwing her head back violently, foaming at her mouth, writhing around in the bed with stiffened chest just minutes before. It was hard to believe that this was not just a bad nightmare and that everything would soon return to how it had been before.

It wasn't just OCD. It was the urgency. The screaming. The hitting and biting, herself and others. It was heartbreak almost every day. One night, "red cookie" was the main subject. It was late, but Lina wanted to go out again for another walk, although she was in no condition for it She was roaming around the apartment like a trapped wild animal. Her body was completely disorganized, arms and legs seemingly oblivious to the rest of her body. Her movements were jerky, her head flailing as if it weren't really attached to her spine. She ran into the playroom, grabbed a thick, hardcover book from the shelf, and threw it. I am not sure if she had intended to throw it at me or if I was just in the wrong place at the wrong time, but it landed hard on my forehead. I screamed out in pain, and Lina screamed even louder. She banged her own head. She bit her own arm. I tried to grab her and hold her down on the soft mattress, but she was all muscle at this point and a little taller than I and she got away. Before I had a chance to catch her again, she bit right into my bicep. Blood immediately surfaced, and it felt like the ligament was detaching from the muscle. I ran right into the kitchen, shrieking from pain. I grabbed an icepack and called Tony to ask him to pick up Elsa, who was crying in her room. It was going to be a long night.

By the time Tony came around, the storm had settled. I felt some kind of numbness, as if I weren't really there. As if all the scratches and wounds and black-and-blue marks on my tired body were not mine, not part of my life, just some kind of mistake, a misunderstanding. Lina is always very calm after the storm. It is as if her episodes were part of a consciousness that she can't access when she isn't in the crisis. If that is true, I see it as a blessing, even if that means my daughter goes in and out of altered states. Before Tony brought Elsa with him to his apartment to protect her sleep and sanity for the rest of that night, the four of us sat in the kitchen, drinking chamomile tea. There were no more episodes that night, and an hour later Lina was sleeping peacefully in her bed.

A couple of days later, Lina's homeotoxicologist, Mary Coyle, called. Mary has been our most valued support ever since we moved back to New York City in 2008. With homeopathic remedies and gentle, detoxing drainage drops, lots of hearty engagement, remarkable intuition, and a uniquely upbeat attitude, Mary helped Lina go from having pretty frequent seizures to almost none. This time, Mary called me to say: "Helena, she has PANDAS, I think you should talk to Dr. Trifiletti." I had called Mary the day after Lina's dramatic regression into OCD and agitation, and Mary, after thinking about it, comparing Lina's sudden symptoms to those of so many other children on the spectrum that she comes into contact with through her clinic, thought Lina's difficulties were very likely PANDAS-related.

Dr. Rosario Trifiletti is a pediatric neurologist who opened his own PANDAS/PANS institute in New Jersey to focus on helping kids suffering from these complex disorders. PANDAS (Pediatric Autoimmune Neuropsychiatric Disorder Associated with Streptococcus) can happen to any child following a strep infection but, for whatever reason, often occurs in children with autism. Following a strep infection, the immune system recognizes the foreign cells, produces antibodies, and attacks the bacteria, but because of the way the strep molecules hide by mimicking host cells in the brain and heart, etc., the immune system not only attacks the strep bacteria, but cells in the brain and heart, as well. This is where the neuropsychiatric breakdown happens. In the case of PANDAS and PANS (Pediatric Acute-onset Neuropsychiatric Syndrome), the consequences of this immune system confusion very often result in acute OCD, tics, agitation, violent outbursts, restlessness, loss of appetite, and difficulties sleeping. Sometimes antibiotics help. Sometimes that's not enough and other therapies are tried, including IVIG (Intravenous immunoglobulin), steroids, and plasmapheresis (plasma exchange therapy in which blood is withdrawn from an individual, the liquid portion is removed and replaced, and the blood is transfused back into the person). The idea is to remove the offending antibodies.

The earliest appointment we were able get with Dr. Trifiletti was several weeks away. How would we survive until then? I wondered. I asked Dr. Trifiletti if we could begin antibiotics in the meantime, after having read up on the symptoms of PANDAS and feeling pretty certain this must be what Lina was up against. But he would not prescribe anything until he examined her. I was in a panic. We needed her to be on antibiotics before our visit so that we had a shot at actually getting her there. So, and this, to be sure, is not one of my proudest moments, I rummaged through my medicine cabinet and, miraculously, found a round of amoxicillin. Lina had had secondary pneumonia early that winter, and after trying every natural remedy there was, we succumbed to traditional meds. We had asked the doctor at City MD to prescribe both the liquid and tablet form so that we could research which one would be the least destructive to her gut bacteria. But now, finding the tablets in my own cabinets, I felt triumphant. Lina responded instantly. The next morning, she was much calmer; still OCDing, but out of the war zone. Her calm lasted almost a week, then the effects seemed to wear off and the agony was reentering her system.

Lina's neurologist, recognizing the severity of Lina's breakdown, agreed to prescribe Zithromax instead, a stronger antibiotic, to help us get to the appointment with Dr. Trifiletti without serious harm. In both cases, the antibiotics first brought Lina relief, then, after about a week, made things worse. But we did manage to get there, our babysitter/aid Roshelle, Lina, and I. Dr. Trifiletti ordered more bloodwork before prescribing anything new, and we left his office after a two-hour-long consultation on Lina's current state, her history, and a brief lesson on how OCD works in kids with autism and PANDAS. Dr. Trifiletti, a large man with polite, soft-spoken manners, seemingly lost in his own thoughts of causes and cures, infections, viruses, transfusions, recoveries, and regressions, struck me as a scientist much more than a doctor. Someone with an open but very busy mind, someone who devoted his life to strange and relatively unknown pediatric neuropsychiatric disorders. I left feeling hopeful that he might help us get a little closer to the enigma of Lina, why we lost her, how we could get her back.

Driving back home from New Jersey, that sense of hope soon turned back into disbelief. Lina began to obsess about "yellow cookies." She began to shriek, her jaw tightened, her legs and arms grew so tense there seemed to be no fluid matter, no blood, no water flowing inside her skin. Her face was pale, her eyes stared into an agonizing nothingness. She kicked me from the backseat. A hard, well-directed kick right into the side of my neck. I looked frantically for an exit. She screamed, "yellow cookies, YELLOW COOKIES!" while foaming at the mouth. I pulled into the parking lot of a McDonald's and quickly got out of the car. Lina struggled to get out. Whenever she falls apart in this way, I search for the softest location for her fists, feet, and head to land. I held her down into the soft backseat while gesturing to Roshelle to stay out of reach of her powerful kicks. Lina wanted to get out of the car, but to try to hold her down on the hard asphalt of this, thankfully empty, parking lot was not an option. So Roshelle and I did our best to hold Lina down against the seat. She was so strong. All muscle. At some point, she got out of my grip and got a hold of one of Roshelle's braids. She pulled hard before I managed to press her hands in toward Roshelle's head and loosen her powerful grip. Tears were burning in the corners of my eyes.

"Roshelle, please, take a break, go, please, I can do this, please don't let her hurt you," I begged with my broken-up voice. Seeing someone you love hurting someone else you love is painful. "Please, Roshelle, let me do this." Roshelle got out of the backseat and right into the front seat, showing no intention to go take a walk or leave us to our predicament. Lina's body softened for a moment, and Roshelle grabbed my shoulder and looked straight at me.

"Helena, listen to me, I am not going anywhere. I am here, I am with you, and we are going through this together. You are my family."

I stared at this beautiful, 26-year-old woman looking at me with her big, faithful, brown eyes, ready to stay in the midst of the most overpowering tornadoes, in the most compromising of situations. How did she develop such an unbending loyalty to us? Her face showed nothing but commitment and love.

"Thank you, Roshelle. Thank you so much. I love you. Thanks for being here with us."

The storm subsided and we drove home. I asked Roshelle to drive and sat next to Lina in the backseat. Lina looked at me and smiled. She talked about this and that but without OCDing. I wondered how it was possible that any human being could be in such dramatically different states from one minute to the next. How far away Lina's ear-deafening screams, tight fists, and powerful kicks seemed in this moment. What was happening to her?

Days, weeks, and months of "yellow cookie, yellow cookie, yellow cookie," "green cupcake cookbook, pink cupcake book," "blue crackers," "I want to hear 'I still love you' (Sting's "A Thousand Years"), can I please hear 'I still love you!', I want to hear I still loooove you! na naaa, naaaa, naaa!" "'Who Says' (Selena Gomez) on the computer, I want to hear 'Who Says' on my computer! blue cinnamon buns!" "pink magazine, I want pink magazine! pink magaziiiine!" Screaming, hitting, kicking, black-and-blue marks, fat lips, scratches, open wounds. Tears, anxiety, anger, rage. Numbness, disbelief, exhaustion.

The first night back in New York City after Fire Island, Elsa went to Tony's apartment and Lina stayed with me. Erika, who had been with us in Fire Island, had one more day with us, so the three of us decided to take a long evening walk. If long enough, this is one of the few things that seems to make it possible for Lina to eventually settle down enough to fall asleep. It was Friday night and we crossed Broadway, Amsterdam Avenue, and Columbus Avenue, talking, walking, singing. Lina obsessed about this or that, and Erika and I joined her the best we could.

> **L:** Yellow cookie. Ye-llow-coo-kie.
> **H:** I hear you.
> **L:** Can I please have a yellow cookie.
> **E:** You do want a yellow cookie. They are yummy.
> **L:** Yellow cookie, yellow cookie, ye-llow-coo-kie!
> **H:** You know I think we can make yellow cookies at our next celebration. My birthday is coming up. Then Elsa's. We can have yellow cookies then if you'd like.
> **L:** Yellow cookie.

Another five minutes of yellow cookie talk, and Lina fell into quiet. We walked into Central Park. There were only a few bikers and a couple on a bench, other than the three of us. On our way back, Lina wanted to go to Papa's house. She wanted the blue cupcake book. The discussion quickly turned tense. We passed by Elsa's old school, PS87. Lina banged on the doors to the empty lobby. She pulled on the door handles. She wanted to get inside at any cost.

Explanations about why that wouldn't be possible at this time were completely futile. Lina's body was getting increasingly stiff. Her voice was becoming shrill. "I want to go that way to Papa's house! Blue cupcake book!" We got away from the school and onto Amsterdam Avenue. Lina took a few jerky steps and then sat down screaming. She banged on the wall of a funeral home. I asked Erika to step aside so as not to get hurt and held Lina from behind. She was kicking and screaming, flailing her strong arms, throwing her head backward to resist the restraint. I brought her down to the ground, sitting behind her, holding her, quietly trying to find the stillness inside the eye of the storm, staying away from my own thoughts, looking for my heart, looking for the stillness that I knew was in there, is always there waiting for me. Lina kept screaming out for Papa's house and the blue cupcake book, yellow cookies, and pink ones. In the outdoor cafés on Amsterdam, people stopped eating. Some stood up, taking their cell phones out, as if wondering if they should call 911. A gang of teenage boys on bikes stopped their bikes, and one boy asked me, "Can we help?" "Thank you, I'm ok, we'll be ok."

Two women outside an ice cream parlor down the street walked over to where I still silently held Lina from behind as she sat squirming, kicking, and shrieking on the sidewalk. They were a little tipsy. The blonde one, wearing a little pink dress and lots of makeup, turned to Lina and asked, "Is she your mother?" I looked at her in disbelief. Erika stepped in and started explaining the situation. Neither the blonde nor her friend was satisfied. "Well, you're disturbing the entire block."

"Lady, please, I'm busy."

"How do I know you're her mother?"

"You're gonna have to take my word for it . . ."

Reluctantly, the two women walked away. I thought about what to do next. We were on 76th Street and Amsterdam, a couple of blocks away from home. Over the summer, Lina had suddenly gotten taller than I, and was so strong. I lifted, carried, and dragged her down the street. We were both drenched in sweat from the struggle. I did not say a word. I just focused on getting the job done. Eventually, we managed to get home. By 1:00 a.m., Lina was asleep. Another day had passed. As I sank down on my own bed, thoughts of leaving the city, taking Lina to a place where she could have her breakdowns on soft grass, under big, comforting trees, away from judgment and drama, seemed like our only hope.

Lina and I were hanging out in the playroom one late summer evening before her bedtime. Suddenly her brain jumped into OCD mode. It was about ice cream in the kitchen. Lina ran into the kitchen and flung open the freezer door. I tried to stop her with words, but Lina was not ready for explanations. She was not in control of any of her impulses. I somehow managed to lift her out of the kitchen and onto the big, soft carpet in our living room. I held my kicking, screaming, adrenaline-stoked daughter down the best I could. I used all my strength to keep my tall, muscular girl on the carpet, dodging her attempts to bite me. She managed to get one of her arms free, grabbed my hair, and pulled as hard as she could. I tried to move in the direction of her pull and loosen her fingers around my hair but felt a hard jab, her other arm free, at the back of my head. She was now out of my grip and up on her feet. I quickly moved behind her, lifted her up, and got her down on her stomach back on the soft carpet. The struggle went on and on, with no sign of slowing down. Lina was in such disarray that she peed on herself while struggling to get out of my grip. I kept holding her as tightly as I could with every ounce of strength that I had left, while softly talking to Lina.

"Lina, I am holding you down until you can hold yourself. I will let you go as soon as your body is calm."

"KITCHEN!!!!!" she screamed. "CHOCOLATE ICE-CREAAAAM!!!!"

The night seemed endless. Both Lina and I were dripping sweat. We had now both lost control of our bladders. It was the lowest and most unprotected I have ever felt. When the storm finally calmed, all I could do was to change both of our clothes, and with a voice that didn't seem to have any tone in it, I asked Lina to go to her bed.

I looked at her, lying there under her thick blanket, with eyes that didn't see. I felt nothing, as if someone had simply removed my heart and all my feelings and sensations and put them in another room. I sat at the edge of her bed, quietly, empty, with nothing more to offer than simply sitting there. Lina looked at me; there was compassion in her eyes. Love.

Awareness. She said:

"There is nothing at all to worry about. There is nothing to go away."

And of course, she is right. There is nothing to worry about. Nothing to judge. Nothing to regret. No elaborate stories to get stuck in. No dreary conclusions about how these are dark, heartbreaking times no matter how you interpret it. How this is inhuman, too terrifying, too overwhelming, too this, too that. It just is. And all I can offer Lina and myself is the love that connects us to each other and to ourselves and to everything alive. And that love will heal every wound, dissipate every sorrow, melt every fear. Love is what will force whatever it was raging in her system to back down, defeated, disarmed. Love will allow Lina peace of mind, flowing, free thoughts, and ongoing joy and well-being.

That's how I talk internally. This is me sweet-talking myself. The idea that love is stronger than any suffering. The idea that's not really an idea but something beyond that, beyond thoughts and feelings and concepts, that we can welcome everything. Regret nothing. When those thoughts run through my head, my mind quiets down, and I find balance and calm. And that is what I am actively looking for in these trying times. I try to eat well, while at the same time pack in as many calories as I have time for and sleep as much as possible whenever I am not up late with Lina. And I do yoga and jump rope and bike every chance I get. To me, it's not about looks and it's not about weight. It's about keeping my body strong in order to keep my mind balanced. With that idea, I started to box.

Whenever someone hears about me boxing, they look knowingly at me and say something about "a good outlet." Sure. But actually, I don't do it because I have some pent-up anger that needs to come out. Boxing to me, more than anything, is improving the quality of my own thoughts and actions. Well actually, the most important reason is that it's fun. It requires all my attention, and I drop everything else to try to memorize the next combination. Jab, cross, slip, slip, uppercut, hook, high change . . . it's a kind of "drop everything and be here and now" remedy. And it teaches me to act with less impulse and more deliberation. To know my surroundings and to know my own place in those surroundings and to learn how to act with intention and thoughtfulness.

My trainer, Roger Grand, whose office is located in Harlem, in the northern parts of Central Park, is the most patient man alive. He is acutely observant and systematic in his teaching. And instead of getting irritated when I go into my dyslexic confusion five drills in a row, he just laughs. Every student gets a different, individualized lesson. Mine is thinking before acting. Don't use up energy that doesn't need to be used up. Wait. Breathe. Without saying anything that can be construed as advice, with nothing much more than a couple of good hugs and eyes that communicated some kind of understanding in spite of the fact that his life experience had very little of Lina's kind of struggles in them, Roger was the one who convinced me to go for my next week long of NeuroMovement training in San Francisco.

NeuroMovement, in addition to marathon walks and ketogenic diet, has been the third trick up our sleeves in helping Lina through this crisis. For the past two years, I've been going to Nevada and San Francisco to train with Anat Baniel, who studied with and eventually became a colleague of Moshe Feldenkrais, who made some of the first revolutionary discoveries within the field of neuroplasticity. The fundamental idea of NeuroMovement is that our brain is an information system that always strives to put order into the disorder, within every area of our functioning, feeling, sensing, and being. According to this method, movement is the main source of information to the brain and helps the brain to form, grow, and organize itself. The brain, through movement, gains the ability to organize all of our movements, thoughts, feelings, and actions and leads us from the impossible to the possible, and to healing. Anat Baniel has taken NeuroMovement to the next level. Her work with athletes, musicians, individuals with cerebral palsy, and special needs children including kids on the spectrum is magical. Training with her has been transformational on every level. Up until Lina's sudden breakdown in early May, the benefits from this work were obvious, from the first time she met Anat in her hotel room in New York City, to our ongoing sessions at home, with me as the practitioner-in-training.

During the past month's acute breakdown, I'd done very little NeuroMovement with Lina. She was in such disarray it didn't seem possible. I was very reluctant to leave her for my next training at the height of her OCD struggles. It felt so wrong to leave her behind. But my boxing trainer saw through that fear and said, "Well if you do go, things will just have to work out, wouldn't they?" "So you're saying I should go?" "No I was just saying *if* you go."

I did go. Something about the idea that things will keep moving whether I am there to watch over them or not helped me remember that I am not indispensable. No one is. And thinking that we are gets us into trouble.

When I got to the training, on a Saturday morning at the beginning of July, Anat looked at me as I was getting ready to go into the first lesson.

"What's wrong?" she said.

"We think Lina has PANDAS."

"Oh, no, I am so sorry."

"I just want to go home . . . I don't want to be here."

"Oh, no, you're not going home. You'll stay here, you'll get some rest, and then you'll go back and help her."

* * *

And that's what I did. I stayed the whole week of training, slept nine hours a night, and came back ready and available to help Lina. Anat encouraged me to keep trying to do a few minutes of NeuroMovement here and there to help Lina through her crisis. I also started Lina and myself on the Ketogenic Diet. High protein, high fat, very few carbs. We wanted to try to address the chronic inflammation in Lina's gut and brain, over-proliferation of yeast, and dramatically fluctuating insulin levels. The first few days on the diet Lina's food obsessions, if possible, escalated. She asked for every little thing she used to have on her normal gluten-free, casein-free, corn-, soy- and mostly sugar-free diet—banana chips, berries, apples, brown rice toast, hot dogs, rice, bananas, apple chips. I was so hungry and tired the first days on the diet, I thought I might be getting sick. But on the fourth day, I felt better. Lina's fourth day seemed better, too. Her OCD episodes did not always lead to mayhem. There were moments, minutes, eventually hours where OCD was no longer at the forefront of her brain. She slept better. We walked everywhere. From school to home. From home to school.

We still sent Lina to the Atlas School downtown. I don't think many other schools would be prepared to handle the acute effects of Lina's breakdowns. But Amanda and Alison and the rest of their team dived right in, headfirst, supporting Lina through endless breakdowns during this heartbreaking period, never once implying that the situation was too much for any one of them to handle. When Lina was falling apart, they would bring Lina into the sensory gym where there were soft mats until the storm settled.

Tony and I decided that for the time being, with Lina's difficulties sleeping and multiple breakdowns, it was best to have the girls sleep in separate places. Lina stayed every other night with Tony during this period; Elsa stayed where Lina wasn't. We tried to protect her the best we could. At Fire Island, Elsa had spent most of her time with our friends' families. As soon as Lina had started to scream, Elsa would hop on her little rental bike and go to Maya's or Anna and Hunter's house. In the city, our every-other-night policy kept Elsa safe and assured her a good night's sleep each night. And in the midst of a difficult night, I had the comfort of knowing that I would sleep the very next night. Tony ordered ketogenic cookbooks, and Elsa and I started to make things happen in the kitchen. Coconut-oil-based chocolate, vanilla and chocolate ice cream, keto bread, and keto scones. We filled the freezer.

The first time Lina took a bite of the keto chocolate ice cream, a smile broke out on her face. She chuckled. Took another bite. Chuckled some more. She ate the ice cream in such a leisurely way, with so much joy and wonder. It seemed that we were onto something here.

Her obsessions began occurring with less frequency. She would drink chocolate smoothies, made with Tibetan mushroom yoghurt and coconut oil and sweetened with a drop of stevia, with so much delight I had to look at her twice to believe what I saw. Sometimes, she even fell asleep before midnight. On her nights with Tony, he would take her on marathon walks from the Upper West Side to Battery Park and back again. Things were still tough, but not as rough as before we tried the ketogenic diet.

Then there was the morning when Lina left the house smiling. I had woken up before Lina and done my half hour of NeuroMovement on her before beginning our day, as she was slowly waking up. On this particular morning, August 29, 2016, as Lina slowly came to life, her obsessions, this time regarding the yellow cupcake book, came along as usual. But instead of just repeating those intrusive, relentless thoughts, Lina, writhing around restlessly on her bed, just said:

"No! No." She waited a little while, then repeated, "Yellow cupcake book."

"Lina, I hear you, you want that book. You have a hard time thinking about anything else.

It seems like it would help you, but that's not it." She looked at me. Normally there would never be this pause. She would not have enough space in her brain to welcome any other thought than the obsession itself. But now, she looked at me, almost curious, as if she wanted me to continue my rambling. Encouraged, I continued.

"We all think the answer is somewhere outside."

"Outside."

"Yeah, we think it's about the cookbook. But it's not. It's inside. We have the answer inside."

"It's outside."

"I know, it feels like it's on the outside, and we all feel that in one way or the other. We think what we are looking for is out there, in a cookie, in a cookbook, in something else that's not us, but it's not true."

"We think it's outside."

"Yes, my love, we do think so. And it makes us miserable . . . but it will pass. The thought will pass."

"It will pass." Lina's face brightened for a moment, then it tensed up again. "No!"

"The thought is back. I know, but eventually it will pass. You'll see, you'll be smiling again. It will pass."

Lina whimpered.

"I know, so hard. If you want you can cry or scream. You can let it out, it's ok." Lina tried to cry. A couple of times. Whimpers came out, but no tears.

"It will pass," she said, her face softening again.

We went to have an egg in the kitchen. Tony came by to drop Elsa off and take Lina to school before I had to get dressed to see a young NeuroMovement client who had found herself in a selective mutism state. Tony waited on the bench outside my apartment door. Lina was in the kitchen. I was preparing myself to have to break the news to Lina that this was the last fried egg she could have before going to school. I was ready to deal with it and then shake it off, like a dog after a swim in the lake. How many fried egg breakdowns we've had even after the second and third and fourth egg is more than I care to recall. As predicted, Lina asked for another fried egg.

"Lina, you will have the rest of your eggs when you get to school." Lina smiled. I stared at her. She smiled, stood up, and walked out to sit down on the bench next to Tony. She looked at me and smiled.

"Fried eggs at school."

We had turned a corner.

The next day was the long-awaited phone conversation with Dr. Trifiletti to discuss the results of Lina's bloodwork. We desperately hoped to find out something concrete about what Lina had been going through for the last couple of months and, possibly, even learn how that may be connected to her sudden regression at three-and-a-half-years old. Before our phone conversation, Dr. Trifiletti emailed me an explanatory spreadsheet and commented, "The results are clear-cut; she has acute mycoplasma infection." Not knowing anything about this infection, I felt like it was a revelation to know something as concrete as this about what was going on with Lina. So many years of questions leading to an infinite number of more questions. So much guessing. And here, we had finally found a doctor who had detected a very elevated count of a bacteria in Lina's blood that has a reputation for interfering with the function of many of its host cells. Bill Welsh, on the Age of Autism website (www. ageofautism.com), describes the mycoplasma bacteria with particular clarity:

"Mycoplasmas are an incredibly malicious and virulent species of bacteria and are not only extremely clever, they are very difficult to trace. Also, it is most likely that should mycoplasma enter the human body's bloodstream they will over time invade virtually any cell they choose, causing a 'gradual deterioration' in the patient. And no doubt, like other pathogens, they will target cells (favored locations) in the host, e.g., the auditory tract, the gut, and the CNS."

The reason these bacteria are so difficult to trace with standard blood tests is that the bacteria lacks a cell wall. Because it doesn't have a cell wall, it's often unaffected by common antibiotics like penicillin, which focuses on bacteria with cell walls. Because mycoplasmas don't have cell walls, they can hide inside the cells of a person or attach outside of those cells and compete with the host cells for nutrients such as cholesterol and amino acids. As host cells do not get the nutrients they need, cell function is compromised. Mycoplasmas are a well-known contaminant of vaccines, but because of the organism's sneaky character, it's very difficult to trace.

The link between the common symptoms reported in children with autism and those of a mycoplasma infection, including but not limited to auditory processing difficulties, language and social challenges, bowel disorder, mitochondrial malfunction, reflux, and Crohn's disease, is becoming increasingly explicit. Bill Welsh hypothesized in his 2015 scientific paper, "Mycoplasma fermentants and deciliation as a precursor to Regressive Autism," which appeared in *Swift Journal of Medicine and Medical Sciences*, that the possibility of vaccines such as measles being contaminated with mycoplasma fermentants may explain why kids become ill, have auditory processing disorders, gut issues, etc., and regress into something that we have gotten accustomed to calling autism directly after receiving their MMR and other vaccines.

Dr. Trifiletti felt that the antibiotic Minocycline would be the most effective in treating Lina's mycoplasma infection and have the advantage of being free of sulfa, which Lina had showed sensitivity to in the past. In light of Lina's acute discomfort while on Zithromax, Tony and I decided to learn more about mycoplasma infection and PANS/PANDAS before exposing Lina to any new medication. Our motivation was strengthened by Lina's recent improvement while on the ketogenic diet. She was indeed having increasing periods without OCD episodes. And when she did have them, they didn't always end up in complete breakdowns. No sugar and an extremely limited carb intake; long walks to and from school, from the Upper West Side to 28th street and back; and more frequent NeuroMovement lessons in the mornings, as Lina was waking up and was still peaceful enough to allow them, were all beginning to help. Lina was smiling more often. She seemed more connected whenever she wasn't stuck in a loop of obsessive thought. She slept a little better. There were alternative routes. We decided to take our time learning what we could do with herbal medicine and biomedical remedies before going back to another round of antibiotics.

I set up an appointment with Geri Brewster, a well-respected nutritionist within autism circles with three decades' worth of experience with the ketogenic diet and kids on the spectrum.

From her, I learned that we weren't really doing the ketogenic diet, but, rather, the modified Atkins diet. It was "modified" in that we were not counting calories. We packed all the calories into Lina's diet that we possibly could, but we didn't give her more than fifteen grams of carbs a day, so even vegetables were limited to a cup at lunch. Nuts, as high in fat and protein as they are, still had to be counted out at snack time. But she could have unlimited naturally cured bacon, chicken, red meat, eggs, oil, oil, oil. Particularly coconut oil, because coconut oil actually creates ketones, and ketones are what we want. Geri taught me how to keep track of whether Lina was producing enough ketones by using keto strips to test her urine at different times of the day. We want Lina's body to learn, or relearn, how to use fat rather than glucose from carbohydrates for energy. When glucose is limited by restricting a person's intake of carbs, the body breaks down fat and converts fat to ketones, which are used in place of the glucose as an energy source in muscle and brain. When the body is in "ketosis," it is returning to its natural state of relying less on sugar-based energy and more on fat and ketones that are produced in the liver by metabolizing fat for fuel. Improved mood, better sleep, and mental clarity as well as a better-regulated blood sugar and reduced inflammation are just a few of the benefits of being in ketosis. The benefits of this diet have been recognized in the treatment of many neurological disorders. Diabetes, high cholesterol, epilepsy, Alzheimer's, Parkinson's disease, autism, and attention deficit disorder (ADD) are a few conditions in which being in ketosis can help restore lost functions. While there is some new research challenging ideas related to the overproduction of yeast called candida, and pointing toward the importance of having balanced gut bacteria and preventing the overproduction of other bacteria such as clostridiales and bacteriodales in the small intestines that are supposed to be produced in the large intestines, most people still consider a yeast infection to be a common and often chronic condition in kids with autism. As in almost any detox process, things often get worse before they get better. Whether it was the symptoms associated with candida or other bacteria—disconnected laughing, a thin layer of white mucus covering the stool, lots of rubbing of cheeks and jaw on every conceivable surface—we first saw more of it with the change in Lina's diet. At the time, I considered this to be a sign that the yeast was on its way out of her system, known as the die-off effect. Now I know it is more complicated than that. It can be either the candida or some other bacterial imbalance or overproduction that can create hallucinogenic substances, with similar effects to LSD, and produce the behaviors that are so commonly seen in children with autism. Whatever it was, for the first two weeks of Lina's diet, that's what we saw.

Why are children with autism so often affected by bacteria imbalance and overgrowth? It is all related to a compromised immune system. Whether the immune system is weakened by chronic viruses; exposure to chemicals that upset the immune system; general environmental factors affecting the immune system such as toxins and chemicals in the air, food, building materials, vaccines, or an ozone layer depletion; or large amounts of antibiotics to deal with the consequences of the above, the weakened good gut bacteria have a more difficult time keeping the bad bacteria in check. Once the normal flora is compromised, bad gut bacteria can take over and actually double in quantity every thirty minutes. Like an army of increasingly unfortunate news, the bad bacteria produce substances like propionic acid, which creates inflammation that damages the intestines, commonly causing a condition referred to as leaky gut. Without intact intestinal walls that prevent bad bacteria from being released into the bloodstream, inflammation spreads throughout the body and most importantly into the brain, potentially causing brain fog, memory loss, anxiety, OCD, and many more complications.

I could see a lot of this in Lina. She would laugh and act silly relative to nothing or no one in particular, almost as if she were drunk or high. She would rub the side of her jaw and cheeks against her hands or me or anything else she could find. She would often seem to be in a fog. Someplace else. Not here. We have tried many natural, antibacterial, and anti-inflammatory remedies, and after she was on the ketogenic diet for a while, I saw the signs of inflammation in her bowels. This is something a mother of a child with autism thinks about. If her child's stool turns greenish-white in response to a new diet or some other added antibacterial or anti-inflammatory supplements, she may feel hopeful that something is coming out of her child's system, or nervous that something is in there that shouldn't be. It's no doubt a bit of a compulsion. Better bacteria and less yeast means more language, relatedness, calm, and explicitly shared experiences. Two weeks into the new diet, Lina seemed more present and less agitated and caught up in her OCD loops.

To outsmart PANDAS, as well as bacteria as malicious and manipulative as mycoplasma, we couldn't really rely on antibiotics alone, particularly since antibiotics cause more of the bacteria imbalance and candida that we were trying to eliminate. Alongside the Minocycline prescribed by Dr. Trifiletti, which we eventually decided was necessary, we consulted with Stephen Harrod Buhner, author of many books, including *Healing Lyme Disease Coinfections*. We slowly began to introduce tinctures: kudzu, cleavers, lion's mane, passionflower, motherwort, and ashwagandha, just to name a few. And of course, probiotics in between; in our case, it was the most potent Tibetan mushroom yoghurt, which I cultivate in my own kitchen (and keep the excess mushroom that grows in the process in my freezer, ready to give away to anyone who needs to feel better, get pregnant, heal gastrointestinal issues, get rid of yeast, improve their immune system, etc.). Lately, though, some research is suggesting that probiotics may produce more problems with the bacteria than they resolve. We also added drops of CBD, another sacred herb and a cannabinoid, well known for its ability to reduce pain, anxiety, inflammation, etc. Furthermore, we reintroduced inositol, a naturally occurring substance similar but not identical to B vitamins, and with many of the same benefits as medical marijuana. There were many other vitamins and tinctures along the way.

I try everything on myself before giving it to Lina, and one night I needed to decide which variety of medical cannabis drops would be most effective. I was running around in my kitchen trying to get food and supplements ready for a very hungry Lina. I resolved to try four drops of one brand that night and continue my motherly research the next night. I figured four drops would be enough to learn something. I'd smoked marijuana twice in my life, and had had multiple cannabis brownies, and had never felt a thing. But now I optimistically concluded that I was indeed the right person for this investigation. I wanted to get things done. I downed one drop after another, a little too stressed to keep up with the counting and carefully execute one drop at a time. I think it is safe to say that there were more than four drops rolling into my mouth, under my tongue, and my research turned into a quite unexpected drama. Two and a half hours later, as I was swinging Lina in her beloved hammock while listening to Anthony Hamilton's "Sister Big Bone," I felt a wave of numbness, I guess you could call it a buzz, up along the outskirts of my brain. Hmm. The next wave was noticeable all along my spine and neck and again all around the outskirts of my brain. The next wave seemed slightly more intimidating. I sat down. I was beginning to notice a kind of numbness not just through my spine, neck, and brain, but also in my legs and soon also my arms and hands. Now I was beginning to feel what I often feel in small doses when I'm alone with Lina. What if something happened to me? What would happen to Lina if something happened to me? Another wave, and I had to fight to stay conscious. I stood up, trying to fix my eyes on something, reached for the phone, and called Tony. "Hey please get here as soon as you can I feel like I'm about to pass out."

"What's happening? I'm putting Elsa to bed, I'll be there soon."

"No, no, now, please now. Drop everything."

Tony got his father to come to his apartment to stay with Elsa, and then his brother to relieve his father. The rest happened without much deliberate action on my part. There was the moment of reading a book with Lina while a Raheem DeVaughn CD played, when I noticed Tony's voice in the music. Wow, Tony has a voice like Raheem DeVaughn—so talented, I was thinking to myself. Who would have known? Lina had an episode, and I just lay there as she stomped around obsessing about "yellow ice cream" in the freezer. She already had her fifteen grams of carbohydrates and a big dinner of chicken in lots of spicy coconut oil sauce, so the kitchen was closed. Her agitation escalated, and I heard myself saying to Tony, "Please protect me." I felt so exposed lying there, noticing the waves coming and going, noticing how some things seemed to come together in my brain and other things seemed to come apart. Lina, miraculously, fell asleep. Tony and I went to my living room. He sat down on the couch holding his head, stressed, discombobulated, not ready to face this unnecessary crisis in the midst of all our current obligatory duties. I stood in the middle of the living room floor trying to say something about life. I looked at Tony's tired, skeptical face and recognized that whatever I had attempted to say had not gone over well. I felt like I should have been wearing a long skirt, lots of scarves, big hoop earrings, and a pair of Birkenstocks as I stood there, trying to make sense of the whole world. Tony shook his head and began to discuss our failed marriage and reasons why it failed. I found it utterly comical that this was the topic of the night and laughed uncontrollably. I found the whole scenario, the drops, Lina, the unprotected nature of my life, Tony's stress, my stress, everyone's stress, unimaginably funny and broke out in one laughing spell after another. Tony looked at me with despair.

"Go home!" I pleaded, in between my laughing fits, "I'm totally fine, everything is fine, go home get some sleep!"

"Please be quiet; you're a mess!"

"No, I am not, I'm good. Don't do that thing."

I was searching for the words to describe "that thing" but found nothing.

"Don't do that thing you do. Just go home."

I woke up the next morning with a new respect for going slow. One drop on Lina's wrist. Wait and see. Next day, another drop. Watch her reaction. One drop under the tongue. Do that for a couple of days. Slow. Steady. Respecting her sensitivity to everything that's coming her way. Letting her notice, get used to, accept, assimilate. Listening and hearing and waiting. That's the lesson that I learned from my little trip. That was, after all, very good research.

Right before Lina's breakdown into obsessive, repetitive land at the end of May of 2016, we had seen so much more creative language, ease with transitions, and ability in Lina to participate more and more fully with everyone around her. Her language was increasingly becoming an expression of herself. There was humor. Much more back-and-forth. Right before her first major OCD episode, the "red-and-black night," as I refer to it, Lina woke up early, walked into my room, smiled, and lay down next to me. Still drowsy, I turned in toward the wall to catch some more sleep. Lina had a different idea of what was important at that moment.

"Everybody needs a group hug."

This was new. Since her regression at 3½, I had never heard Lina actively ask for a hug. Most of the time, she had just seemed to accept that people around her needed to hug her. I hugged her and tried my best not to overwhelm her with the sudden rush of joy that her words had evoked. Later on, I left Lina in the playroom (which is what we all call Lina's room) to go make some coffee. On my way to the kitchen, the couch spoke to me and I sank into it. Five minutes later, Lina came after me, smiling, and sat down next to me. I hugged her and said, "Du ardet finaste som finns," which is Swedish for "You are the most wonderful thing that exists." Lina, again, completely blew my mind.

"I am glad to hear that," she said.

During this same period of dramatically improving language and active manipulation of her world via language, Lina again came into my room one early morning. This time, she wanted my bed to herself, pushed me gently away from herself, and said:

"Go wash your body."

I wasn't having it, not ready to leave the warm bed behind, and told Lina that this is my bed and the only bed she could push me out of was her own. Lina wasn't convinced, thought about it, and then said:

"Go make coffee."

I smiled as I left to make my favorite drink of the day, thinking about how much processing and emphatic connection this comment had revealed.

Even after the breakdown at the end of spring, I had the feeling that, while the OCD and everything that came with it overshadowed most moments, underneath it was a girl growing to become a woman. Beneath all the repetitive and escalating drama was a person who was beginning to learn and relearn how to think about herself and other people. Someone with personality and awareness. Someone who has so much to say but doesn't know how.

CHAPTER TWO

Energy Workers and
Our Farm in the Country

W HEN ELSA ENTERED middle school, we sought a
new pediatrician, which led us to an open-minded,
spiritually connected doctor, who, when he heard
about Lina, not only gave us information about raw milk, better
butchers, Native American clay, and the book *How Do You Hug
a Porcupine?* by Laurie Isop, but he also gave us the number for
Barbara Wosinski, a psychic energy worker. And as I wrote to
her about Lina, I simply recollected Lina's regression; told her
about the mycoplasma infection, the acute OCD, and breakdowns; and asked if there was anything else I could do to help

her through. During our hour-long phone conversation, without knowing anything else about Lina, Barbara described how important color was to Lina; how she thinks in color; how blue or purple are good colors for helping her calm down; how room temperature food is better for her than hot food; how she responds to music, water, foot rubs, and lower back rubs; how she misses her little sister Elsa when she is not around but that our arrangement, splitting them up for part of their week, works perfectly. Without having met Lina, it was definitely my daughter this remarkable woman, with her thick Midwestern accent, described. The one thing that was obvious but was becoming increasingly urgent was Lina's need to talk. Barbara referred to it as "too much energy in her head." Lina wants to speak and has a lot of things to say, Barbara told me. Never before has the discrepancy between Lina's maturation and awareness and her expressive language ability been more dramatic. She speaks in color, but no one, or at least no one we know, sees the world in this way. So where is the bridge between her world and mine? How can I help my daughter find her words? How can I learn to understand her? She so clearly doesn't need reassurance. She doesn't want to be distracted or manipulated. She wants to be understood.

For a long time, I had been thinking about taking Lina out of the city and into nature, at least for part of the week. For someone as sensitive and open as Lina, so much of her energy and focus is spent trying to negotiate the overwhelming stimulation of a big city. All the agenda, the aggression, the aggravation. The stress, the struggle for space. The fight for success. And so I began a search for a country place. I walked in and out of houses in every county in upstate New York without finding home. Sometimes Lina and Elsa came with me. Most of the time, I traveled on the days they were both in school or when they were at Tony's house. Then one day, when winter was still holding spring at bay, I walked into the house in North Salem, an hour away from New York City. It had a main house and a guest house. It also had a barn and a high-ceiling studio where I immediately imagined the girls jumping on a big trampoline and swinging on swings and hammocks and climbing and balancing and having fun indoors in the middle of cold winters. I imagined the barn harboring goats and chickens, and maybe even a horse or two. I imagined a dog on the front porch, kids swimming in the large pool that we would convert to a saltwater pool as soon as the next spring came around. I imagined swings everywhere on the five-and-a-half-acre property and a treehouse where a child or two could hide away from adults and share some secrets. I stood on the porch and felt the wind from the large open field in front of the house and thought, *this could be the end of my search*. It had everything. Space, land, separate buildings for fun and for animals and for visitors. While only an hour away from the city, here were woods, birds, wildlife, and lots of untouched land all around. The house and the space around it were quiet, but not so quiet that city people would freak out. There was a nearby lake and a neighbor, a policeman from Yonkers who, as it turned out, said it would be no problem for us to make a path on the side of his property to walk over to Peach Lake.

It was a run-down house with a run-down roof and old windows that the wind had no trouble blowing right through. The yellow-and-red lead paint was peeling, and inside many of the ceilings was water damage. But it was a beautiful, charming old house with thick, old trees and open fields and pasture all around it. The way I saw it, it had endless potential.

I split it with Tony 50/50. Is it a good idea to buy a country house with your ex-husband? Well, it was the only way that made this purchase possible, so I didn't spend a whole lot of time pondering the question. I knew I would need that energy to figure out how to make the house livable. Tony and I closed in June 2016, and I moved in one sunny afternoon in October that same year. It was just me and a bunch of moving guys. And when they left, the house seemed so quiet that I could hear ringing in my ears. Maybe my ears had been ringing for years and I just hadn't noticed. The city is always full of noise. Out here, I felt like I could hear my own thoughts move. It was bewildering. The first night I stayed over in the house was so unsettling that I stayed awake for almost the entire night. I wanted to leave but felt like I had to stay. As if I had to initiate the house. But there was something in the house. I felt it. Something was hovering there. I burnt wild sage incense every chance I got, walking with the soft smoke from room to room.

When I took Lina with me for the first time after moving in, she did not want to go into the house. "Go Home," she kept saying and sat in the car for a long time before finally and reluctantly walking through the front door. She clearly felt something, too. She was very unsettled for the first couple of hours after we got there. The same thing happened the next time we went up there. So now what? I thought about it. And I decided that we all have struggle. Life on Earth involves struggle. People who had been on this land, in this house, had struggled. I'm lucky, I thought to myself, to know that there is something here that I will have to deal with. I turned to Barbara Wosinski for this, as well. I told her what Lina and I had felt and asked her if she could help me clear the land, the house, every space there. She agreed. And a week later, she told me that the land, ours and the neighboring property, had held so many losses from war, starvation, and drought that it was literally sinking in a pool of sorrow. She told me about a woman and two children who had lived on the ground, before the current house was built. They had been very scared and abandoned. She talked about how the house and the porch were leaning forward into the earth because the land had so much pressure and no direction. She said the land wants a direction. It wants children. It wants laughter and playing. It is ready for a new beginning. It will be a very happy place, and it has a good future.

Barbara did her clearing, and the girls, Roshelle, and I went to the house on weekends and some weekdays every now and then. Lina was beginning to enjoy it. "Taking the blue car with mom to North Salem," or simply to "the house" or even "my house," was becoming one of her standard requests. It was fall and getting cold, but Lina and Elsa were swinging on the swings and outdoor hammocks throughout October and November. We had friends and their kids over. We celebrated Thanksgiving up there with Tony, and his whole family—his recently widowed father, one of his brothers, his sister and her family, and a friend—all came up to celebrate with us. And so, the slow process of making this house a home began.

It was so different to look out the windows from the second-floor bedrooms and instead of looming concrete and steel to see a huge field with rolling hills ringed by trees. It was so strange to lie in bed at night, hearing nothing but the soft wind gently rustling the bare branches of the trees outside. One night, I suddenly woke up and thought someone had turned on the light in my room before realizing it was just the full moon shining through our windows. There were no street lights to diffuse the natural light of the moon and the stars. There were very few cars and almost no people to compete with the sound of birds, wind, and silence. Silence is also a sound.

I was beginning to remember my own childhood. While I grew up surrounded by forest and lakes, I had spent most of my adult life in New York City. Apart from her first two years, Elsa had spent all her life in Manhattan. Lina had spent two-thirds of hers in the city. This was going to take some getting used to. While Lina filled up most of our country house days with everything from Stevie Wonder, Sting, Anthony Hamilton, and Tracy Chapman to The Ting Tings, Katie Perry, and Taylor Swift, nothing here was coming at us like it does in the city. It just was. The trees outside the house just stood there. Not welcoming or unwelcoming. They were just there, standing, unassuming, noninvasive, silent.

The day after Thanksgiving, after Elsa and her dance company had danced in the Macy's parade, she experienced such an anticlimax that she suddenly felt a desperate urge to climb something. We had been sitting peacefully in the hay loft of the barn, dangling our feet out the huge attic door while looking out at the field and calculating whether we would actually hurt ourselves if we jumped the three-and-a-half yards down from the attic to the ground, when Elsa insisted on "climbing something." We marched over to the studio that we were in the process of turning into the giant playhouse (or in special ed. jargon, a sensory gym). I had initially envisioned it with an indoor trampoline, swings, mats on the floor, a giant crash mat next to the trampoline, a ping-pong table for bigger kids, boxing bags, etc. Since there was nothing yet to climb on in there, I threw a rope around one of the thick beams that stretched from one side of the building to the other and made a knot halfway up.

"Here, climb!" I said triumphantly.

Elsa wasn't feeling it. She needed a tree. We went out to look for a good climbing tree, but despite all the trees, none appealed. Elsa stomped back into the house. Later, she confessed to not yet knowing what to do with herself in the country.

I think each of us had our own version of this transition. Mine was simply running around in the house, up and down the stairs, forgetting what I was getting, back down, into the kitchen, checking on Elsa up in the attic where she had her art supplies, checking on Lina in the living room, swinging, spinning, and checking out music, running back and forth for the next supplement, back to find Lina and have her swallow whatever supplement was on the schedule with some water, putting up the outdoor hammock swing between two trees in the yard, and shouting to the girls to come out and swing and watch the deer out on the field. Basically, what my life was in the city, but with more stairs and a backdrop of peace and quiet. Lina's version, her process of getting used to this quiet country house, was going between her upstairs room and her books, to the living room and the music, out to the field to the red tire swing. When she got upset, she would go and sit in the car for a while. Possibly scream a little, thrash around, and then come back in the house. We all had our ways to turn this place into something that felt welcoming and familiar, that would help all of us to find peace and our own way of being that didn't require the endless and ongoing stimulation of a big city.

As always, this house was ultimately and foremost our next attempt in an endless myriad of trial-and-error procedures to get our Lina back.

CHAPTER THREE

Safe Vaccines

GET HER BACK from what? you might wonder. If you read my first book, you know more of the details around Lina's early development. How she had developed normally up until age three-and-a-half. Then, on September 20th, 2006, Lina had her second MMR vaccine. Shortly after, she had her first of an endless series of seizures, was drooling for two weeks straight, lost all her speech, became disoriented, and began acting extremely bizarre. Our lives, from then on, were never the same. I wish I had some other story to tell you, because the implications of this story are so tremendous, so unthinkable, so terrifying. I am not against vaccines. I never was and probably never will be. But like hundreds of thousands of other families whose children lost their ability to live comfortably in this world, who could no longer talk or listen, who started to have seizures, scream, bite, hit, and scream, who developed painful gastrointestinal issues and became sensory-craving or sensory-avoidant, who could no longer find peace and harmony anywhere in their lives following their vaccinations, I hope that safe vaccines one day become more important than the profit made by huge pharmaceutical companies, the CDC (Centers for Disease Control and Prevention), the FDA (Food and Drug Administration), and the medical establishment. Because that is all I am asking for. Safe vaccines.

I've never understood why someone who is advocating for safe vaccines will be called an antivaxxer. It's just as unbelievable to me as attacking Native Americans with rubber bullets, bats, gas, and other violent measures in South Dakota, when all these beautiful people want to do is to peacefully protect our water. Why has "safe vaccines" become a curse word? How can we say that we know that vaccines and autism have nothing to do with each other while the government has already paid over $2 billion in compensation to families with vaccine-damaged kids? Why is the CDC, which is awkwardly responsible for both promoting and investigating the safety of vaccines, refusing to compare the development of vaccinated versus unvaccinated children? And why is compensation for vaccine damage the responsibility of the tax payers? Because in 1986, when the numbers of kids on the spectrum began to rise dramatically and families began to try to sue the manufacturer of the vaccines, the Reagan administration came up with the National Childhood Vaccine Injury Act (NCVIA), which relieves the pharmaceutical companies of any financial responsibility for vaccine-damaged children. Instead, the government (or the taxpayer) would pay the families of vaccine-injured kids. Well, until they didn't. Because currently, these families are on their own. The government no longer compensates for this particular damage, because there are simply too many vaccine-damaged kids at this point. In the *Journal of Autism and Developmental Disorders,* December 2018, Volume 48, Issue 12 (McDonald and Paul), the increase in autism rates is undeniable:

"Epidemiologic estimates of autism prevalence in the United States were in the range of 1 in 2500 prior to 1985, but increased to 1/150 among 8-year-olds born in 1992 and again to 1/68 for 8-year-olds born in 2002."

In the CDC's *Morbidity and Mortality Weekly Report*, April 27, 2018, the new autism rate is established. For 2014, the overall prevalence of autism spectrum disorder (ASD) was 16.8 per 1,000 (one in 59) children aged eight years.

The epidemic increase in autism prevalence is consistent with the increase in vaccines as recommended by CDC's vaccine schedule. Many more vaccines were added to the schedule after the passage of the National Childhood Vaccine Injury Act (NCVIA) in 1986 that severely limited the liability of vaccine manufacturers and established the National Vaccine Injury Compensation Program (a.k.a. "The Vaccine Court"). Just how prevalent autism has become is even more difficult to establish after VAERS (Vaccine Adverse Event Reporting System) was created as an outgrowth of the NCVIA and administered by the FDA and CDC. VAERS collects and analyzes data from reports of adverse events following vaccinations. However, it does not require doctors to enter cases. Many doctors are unaware of VAERS, and many doctors won't report suspected injury cases because of fear of professional reprisal. In other words, we don't currently have an effective system in place that can capture the full extent of autism in the US.

Lina still has toxic levels of mercury in her system. She has serious inflammation in almost every organ of her body as well as in her brain. Since we began to understand that our daughter suffers from an overload of toxicity, we began working with Mary Coyle, homeotoxicologist, focusing specifically on detoxifying children on the spectrum, whose organs have shut down under the burdens of heavy metals and other toxins. Under Mary Coyle's guidance, Lina's organs are functioning better and she no longer has regular seizures. But we have a very long way to go, and the government did not pay a penny for this or any of the other treatments we have tried to get Lina back. In the context of all of this, I am wondering when the CDC and the medical community will finally begin to consider breaking up the MMR vaccine into single vaccines. Merck, the pharmaceutical company that has a monopoly on MMR vaccines, does not want to do that, because then they would lose their monopoly. I am also wondering when it will be a good time to consider giving vaccines later rather than earlier, to protect immature immune systems from too much stress, too soon. Why wouldn't we want to find out if it is safer for our infants and toddlers to get their vaccines later? Why do we put up with preserving vaccines that go into our newborns with aluminum and mercury, which are not only extremely toxic by themselves, but together take toxicity to a higher level? Many vaccines are formulated with aluminum in plants that clean their equipment with mercury. Even very small levels of mercury, as little as 2 percent combined with aluminum, become a significant toxicity issue in vaccines.

It is true that mercury, like thimerosal, was removed from most childhood vaccines between 2001 and 2005. Unfortunately, many of those vaccines still contain small amounts of thimerosal. Furthermore, thimerosal is commonly used to clean vaccine manufacturing equipment and components. A new danger among recommended vaccines is the maternal and infant flu shots. The flu shot is not yet on the obligatory vaccine schedule; however, it is strongly recommended by the CDC and FDA for every year of life. What most people are not aware of is that many flu vaccines contain 25 percent thimerosal. In other words, the parent who follows the exact vaccine schedule recommended by their pediatrician may cause their child the same level of mercury toxicity as before mercury was removed from the MMR vaccines.

What is important in the vaccine discussion, I believe, is transparency, and an unbiased organization committed to researching and promoting the safest vaccines possible, regardless of cost. In 2014, a top scientist at CDC, William Thompson, PhD, took an important step in this direction. Thompson went to the public and revealed records that show how the CDC distorted, concealed, manipulated, and omitted research data that show the detrimental effects of the MMR vaccine, particularly for African American boys. In a press release on August 27, 2014, William Thompson made his statement about the 2004 article examining the possibility of a relationship between the MMR vaccine and autism:

"I regret that my coauthors and I omitted statistically significant information in our 2004 article published in the journal *Pediatrics*. The omitted data suggested that African American males who received the MMR vaccine before age 36 months were at increased risk for autism. Decisions were made regarding which findings to report after the data were collected, and I believe that the final study protocol was not followed."

Those fraudulent research results were used by the Department of Justice to deny 5,000 petitioners due process and their children potential compensation in the Vaccine Court autism proceedings. Mainstream media cannot be relied on for objective coverage of vaccine controversies. The pharmaceutical industry, which is the major advertiser on the networks, and the government simply will not accept criticism of vaccine safety. If a top scientist is willing to risk his job and his reputation to alert the public to a fraud that harms our children, why aren't we willing to listen?

I love Lina. I love my life with her. I don't spend much time regretting things but try to focus most of my energy on getting Lina back to the harmonious, bilingual, interactive, compassionate, and cognitively intact child she was before she suffered the severe brain damage caused by her second MMR vaccine. The suffering and challenge that she has been through for almost a decade now are unimaginable. I am hoping that maybe, by telling our story, other families will not have to learn about this in the way Lina, her little sister Elsa, my ex-husband, and I all did. And maybe one day, with so many of us knowing someone with a vaccine-damaged child, that vaccine policy will change. I am hoping that one day, Congress will subpoena Dr. William Thompson to hear his testimony. I also hope that Congress will repeal the 1986 National Childhood Vaccine Injury Act and hold pharmaceutical manufacturers accountable and liable for injuries and suffering caused by their vaccines. Furthermore, I hope that MMR vaccines will become available as separated, single measles, mumps, and rubella vaccines and that the ages at which children are vaccinated are delayed until their immune systems are more resilient. Finally, I hope that all vaccines will be considered pharmaceutical drugs like any other drugs and therefore be required to undergo the same rigorous testing as every other drug.

And no, I do not want to hear from one more official, doctor, president, politician, newscaster, CDC, or FDA official that vaccines are safe. If they are so safe, why wouldn't the CDC or any other governmental agency be willing to compare the autism rates of vaccinated versus unvaccinated children? There is a widespread fear of articulating any criticism regarding vaccines. As an author, I have often been encouraged to delete what I write about vaccines in order to get articles related to autism and healing published. But after what happened to Lina, I am not afraid of what people think and not concerned about being politically correct. I am afraid that more children will suffer the way Lina has suffered and am grateful for the opportunity to tell our story, the way it was.

CHAPTER FOUR

Alternative Paths

L INA IS SO much more than her vaccine damage. Most
of us have discovered that life isn't some linear thing
that makes sense according to a particular pattern. Lina
is a good example of how, in order to understand someone,
one has to approach the person as well as oneself from many
different angles. There are surface stories. Deeper perspectives.
Multidimensional viewpoints. In my work as a psychotherapist,
I know my clients have particular reasons for coming to me.
Someone may have given them a diagnosis along the way—
depression, bipolar disorder, social phobia, trichotillomania,
panic disorder, addiction, borderline personality disorder. They
have had experiences that led up to that diagnosis, and it can be

helpful to know those stories. But if those were the only things I understood about those individuals, I would not be as helpful to them, and my understanding would be extremely limited. The same is true with Lina. If all I saw in her was her limited language, her awkward movements, her outbursts, her sensory craving, her gastrointestinal issues, her mycoplasma infection, I would miss a great deal about her. And in fact, my perception would be limiting not just to me, but to her, too.

Therefore, as I have learned to trust these other parts of Lina, I am careful whom I invite to treat her. Most of the professionals who are helping Lina at this point are connected and aware of energetic reality. Lina's neurologist, Dr. Maya Shetreat Klein, is also a practicing shaman, and cleaning out toxins and inflammation from Lina's various systems is done with candles, incense, and prayers as much as with biomedical remedies.

Lina's homeotoxicologist, Mary Coyle, works from her belief that the energy from minerals, plants, and animals can be trusted to detoxify, soothe, enlighten, clarify, and heal. She exudes hope and positive energy, smiles easily with her dimples showing, and talks with a bright, energetic voice about endless possibilities, the most noninvasive, soothing, and supportive homeopathic allies for Lina's next steps toward healing. Mary never seems to be far away from a little joke or a chuckle and empathizes easily with any child walking through the doors of her colorful, home-like office in downtown Manhattan. She connects effortlessly with parents and caretakers, with the most powerful common denominator: the experience of having a child on the spectrum. Her son is a young adult now, has completed college, and is getting ready to find his way in the world of work but once struggled with the same intense challenges as Lina.

* * *

Stephen Harrod Buhner, author of *Healing Lyme Disease Coinfections,* advises complementary and holistic treatments for bartonella and mycoplasma coinfections. We consulted him about which herbs would most effectively outsmart Lina's particular mycoplasma bacteria. He knows more than anyone I have ever come across about the healing properties of herbs and talks and writes about plants as if they were his close friends, his colleagues, respected for their intelligence and sacred, quiet power.

Most recently, Lina and I met with Marilyn Chadwick, a speech and language pathologist who specializes in augmented communication. I am not sure if she would consider herself spiritual or working with energy, but in my understanding, anyone who spends more time listening, with an openness to the inherent beauty and intelligent of another person, cannot but work with energy. Mary Coyle sends me links to relevant articles and treatment options whenever she comes across something that may be relevant to Lina. Mary suggested we explore Marilyn's computer-aided communication, which helps kids on the spectrum to express themselves through typing. I felt that this kind of alternative communication had limitations. I see the way technology disconnects us from one another rather than how it helps us relate. I see so many kids trapped in front of a computer, overstimulated yet addicted to the virtual world of computers and TV. I suspected a technical approach would be yet another way to lose my connection with Lina. For those reasons, I stubbornly resisted trying Marilyn's method. But Mary kept patiently talking to me about it, and one day in mid-December, the idea of facilitating communication via a computer suddenly didn't seem like such a bad idea. In early January, as Marilyn came to New York to work with a few children at Lina's school, we decided to try it out.

Lina was playing an interactive game in her classroom when it was time for her meeting with Marilyn. She reluctantly sat down on the couch in one of the directors' offices. Lina was tense. She wanted to "go back to the classroom, please." Her desire to leave rather than engage in the simple sequence game on Marilyn's computer escalated, and soon Lina's voice went from talking to shrieking. I went over to the desk and picked up a little pad and a marker. I wrote down all Lina's desires in the way she formulated them and illustrated the words with sketches of what the next couple of hours would look like. I drew a couch with Lina and Marilyn and me sitting in it and typing; the next picture was of Lina back in the classroom; the next, a picture of her and Donovan, our new caregiver who started working with Lina after Roshelle left, walking Lina back to my apartment, etc. Lina engaged enough in this process to bring her voice down to baseline and sit a little deeper into the couch. Marilyn typed "you are a beautiful girl" on the computer and read it out loud, since Lina has trouble with coordinating her eyes enough to follow written texts. She then handed it over to me and asked if I wanted to type something. I typed something about typing and how I was curious about whether Lina wanted to try it.

Instead of typing an answer, Lina clicked a couple of buttons and was suddenly in Marilyn's private photo album. Lina, who loves pictures, browsed through the pictures with increasing ease. Marilyn tried to have her play another sequencing game on the computer, but Lina became anxious and asked about going back to the classroom, going with me in "the blue car," etc.

I got the pen and paper and again showed Lina the simple sketches about what the plan for the day was. This helped Lina feel grounded enough to return to her work with Marilyn. I think the writing and drawing may function as a bridge between concrete and abstract thinking and serves multiple purposes for Lina. For one, writing it down shows Lina that she is being heard, and while what she says is much more limited than what's on her mind, the concrete desires that she does express are recognized and therefore, I believe, easier for her to let go of. For Lina, at that time, the writing and drawing somehow seemed to help her process her OCD anxiety that felt so overwhelming and fragmenting to her. Her words were like unconnected puzzle pieces, and my writing them down and sketching them seemed to help her see the whole picture, to gain perspective, to feel herself in a context. It seemed to help her to calm down enough to allow her to express more complex parts of herself.

Calmer now, Lina typed the following:

L: JjjPPOIIIUUYYYTTIIIIIIIUIIIIUUYYTWQ . . .

Marilyn then supported Lina's right wrist while Lina kept typing:

L: we are playing with Marilyn blue car with Mimi like
red cars too. Please go in the
carGg

I stared at Lina's written words. They didn't make much sense. But they were typed words. I didn't know that Lina could write! I have always recognized that Lina is an aware human being and that her words don't reflect what's inside of her. And of course we have practiced writing, letter recognition, and putting words and sentences together, but the physical act of writing with just a very subtle support under her wrist was miraculous. And what was to come was even more mind-blowing.

Marilyn typed her response while simultaneously reading it out loud:

> **M:** Try to focus on what you might like to say.

Marilyn again gently supported Lina's right wrist as Lina responded:

> **L:** Treating me like a real person is scary I very much like to believe that my life can be good with real things that I sd
>
> **M:** What are some of the real things that you would like in your life?
>
> **L:** Teach others free my voice and help to very much easy say what I am thinking.
>
> **M:** You want to free your voice. You have a lot to say.
>
> **L:** Yes I do. Really trying to give you what you want but I please myself in my mind.
>
> **M:** Do you want to do this?

Lina looked at Marilyn. She looked at me. It was clear that this wasn't a simple question to answer. Her internal world is hers. As Lina wrote, "I please myself in my mind." Her connection with other frequencies, other spaces, is so much more colorful and magical than ours.

Marilyn and I decided to wait for Lina's decision, both trusting that once Lina made up her mind about whether or not to type in this way, she would let us know.

Lina sees things that most other people don't see. She lives in a world that is much more fluid and interesting than the one we are used to calling reality. She is a water child. When she was a baby, I would walk up and down a little beach with her in the sling. She would listen quietly to the water, always at peace near the water. Her mind, I think, is like water. Her thoughts run in unconventional ways. Even when she was a little toddler, before her regression, she seemed to live much more in the oceanic consciousness that some people label as right brain functioning, a sense of oneness with others, a natural wish to give, to love, to see people smile. She was different. I never saw her fighting over toys with other kids in the sandbox. She seemed fully content to share whatever she had. When Lina was a toddler, she and her best friend Ellen went to a preschool for a couple of hours a day. One of those days, a mother who had her son in the same group as Lina came up to my ex-husband Tony.

"Do you have a second?" she asked him, "I just want to talk to you about something."

Tony, who loves to talk about anything between the sun and the moon with whoever is around him, agreed.

"I'm just curious, what do you do with Lina? She is just so incredibly sweet, social, and generous with all the kids, and the relationship she has with Ellen is just incredible. And she speaks so incredibly well! I guess what I am asking is, is there something specific you guys are doing to encourage her to be like that? I would really appreciate any ideas you have about this, I mean anything specific? I would just love it if my son could be more like that."

I have no idea what Tony told this mother. But I do know that what she said to him that day is something he held onto through the years, to remind himself of a part of Lina that seems forever lost after her second MMR vaccine. No one these days comes up to us and talks about how incredibly social and relational and well-spoken Lina is. I used to call her my little Buddha. It wasn't just about the way she sat and the little ripples of fat on her arms and legs and ankles, though she was certainly a substantial baby. But more importantly, her attitude was so relaxed. She seemed to know deeply that she had everything and she didn't need to hold onto anything, she didn't need to fight for things, she was just fine. She loved to play, read, and eat; she loved water, music, people. And all that is still true.

Malidoma Somé, PhD, was born in the village of Dano in Burkina Faso, West Africa. He is an initiated elder, diviner, medicine man, and author of several books such as *Of Water and the Spirit; Ritual: Power, Healing and Community;* and *The Healing Wisdom of Africa.* He lives in Orlando, Florida, but travels around the Western world to do divinations, lectures, and workshops. Tony, Lina, and I met him one spring afternoon in a little basement office in Brooklyn. He did divinations, a kind of ancestral reading, on all three of us. In the small room where he was waiting for us, he had a little round table in front of him with hundreds of shells and stones and other colorful things that he asked Lina to touch and move around. Malidoma believes Lina is a healer who had her shamanic awakening too soon. It became very difficult for her to talk about it in a coherent way. He described her awakening experience as if she were a deer caught in the headlights; she connected with so many frequencies at the same time, and her every neuropathway was on high alert. He described how, even for an adult, the initiation process, the shamanic awakening, can be rough. For Lina, it was so overwhelming that it became extremely disorienting to her.

Malidoma said that most people in a community are not vibrating as easily with other frequencies as Lina does naturally. We all could, I believe, but most of us are too caught up in our mind and emotion to hear and feel what is going on vibrationally all around us. Lina, Malidoma explained, can see thought patterns, or feel them, even without anyone saying anything.

"She sees and feels them as colors, layers of wisdom, layers of knowing, traceable to various sources." Malidoma believes these potential capabilities exist in everyone, but when people are born with all of them activated, they cannot participate in the world as we know it because they know too much:

"It may translate as an oversensitivity . . . but the richness of their world is much broader and she can see the rest of us as quite boring, single-minded, and so simplistic. In another world Lina would be just perfect. Like in a village, with indigenous people, where there is none of the artificiality . . . she would be able to interact with so many things . . . birds! And the little fairies.

"And that's why you can't act toward her as if she has a condition but rather as if you are a student of hers. Then she may reveal a few things to you . . . if you behave right . . . she may fill you in on some hidden reality that she is in touch with because she can hear language on various levels, she can understand the language of animals, she can hear the language of birds, she can feel the frequencies of trees. When she gets a hold of a flower she can feel the frequency of the flower vibrating.

"It's a kind of blessing that normal beings don't know how to relate to. It's a school unto itself. She is in touch with the wisdom of the origin, the kind of wisdom that it will take people years and years to become aware of."

Malidoma pointed at a book Lina brought and continued.

"Everything comes to life for her. She can look at these pictures and trace them down to the person who drew these and begin talking with that person's higher spirit."

Malidoma laughed as he continued to look at the shells and stones and pearls in front of Lina.

"There is so much fluidity . . . everything is dancing, there is a little girl sailing on a little ship in the vast ocean with no destination in mind because the journey is the destination and every now and then there is something like a dolphin with a human head or some kind of unseen entity that comes up and gets into conversation with her. It is so farfetched that is has nothing to do with human reality. She is such a combination of beauty and arts it's like she is Alice in Wonderland or one of the members in the *Chronicles of Narnia* and that's why she is so busy busy all the time."

Malidoma kept staring at her shells in front of her and laughing and chuckling as he tried to describe to me and Tony what he saw in a way that we could comprehend.

"I have never seen anything more complete."

He and Lina looked at each other and smiled. Lina has never liked to be talked about when she is right there. But in this case, as Malidoma described what he saw in her divination, her smile broadened, and she sank deeper into her chair, as if relieved to have her alternative worlds recognized verbally by someone in the world she had so much trouble with.

In spite of her challenges and limitations in the physical realm, Lina certainly feels like a very complete human being. There is the possibility of parents with special needs kids glorifying and exaggerating their offsprings' unseen gifts, sure. As a defense. As comfort. As compensating for their child's disability. But the brain is a complicated thing. Have you ever had an injury, let's say a bad knee, and then you twisted your ankle? And as the ankle began to swell up and cause you great pain, the pain you'd been experiencing in your knee for months magically dissipated? Our brain is registering pain and new neuropathways are formed, and eventually acute pain may turn into chronic pain, because our brain learned to keep up the job of alerting us that our knee hurts. When language and conventional logic and motor pathways are compromised, there is intuition, oceanic love, expansiveness, and creativity in a completely different part of the brain. Maybe that part, which is so connected with everything alive, is less vulnerable to damage or not vulnerable at all. Maybe realizing our connection with one another and everything around us is the single most important component to all healing. Maybe that's where we go when we feel so challenged, so pressed up against the wall that we are forced to take refuge in something greater than what we have become accustomed to calling ourselves.

I do believe that Lina's connectedness is the way she has the ability to see what others don't see, to see colors, to trace thoughts before they've been expressed, to feel the frequency of a flower the way few of us can, to understand a foreign language without having learned that language, to touch someone who needs to be touched, to say something to someone who is losing hope that sounds strange and confusing to anyone except that person, who instantly feels strengthened by her words.

A close friend of mine and her beautiful family were staying in New York for a week for medical reasons related to her son, who has a rare genetic disorder that makes their lives very complicated and challenging. My friend, whom I'll call Sarah, was with Lina in the playroom. I had already explained to my friend that Lina reads people's auras and sometimes talks about it with people she meets. Lina was in her hammock and Sarah was sitting next to her, reading one of Lina's favorite books, *What is*

Love? (written by Dar Draper and beautifully illustrated by Sarah Dawn Helser). Lina looked right at Sarah and said:

"Come out of the black into the orange."

Sarah, like many mothers and fathers with severely challenged children, was fighting to stay out of depression. Lina watched her lovingly from the swing. Tears were falling down my friend's cheeks as she thanked Lina for thinking and caring about her.

Another close friend of mine, "Clarice," called me one day in the early spring of last year. Her voice was broken up not by tears, but by terror. Still in disbelief, I gathered from her incoherent speech that her brother and sister-in-law had both died under horrific circumstances. After our phone call, I turned to Lina.

"Lina, what can I tell Clarice that will help her?"

"Tell her 'I am sorry,'" Lina said and continued flipping through the pages of her book.

Those words turned out to be the most helpful words anyone could have used to comfort my friend. They were central to the situation and central to my friend. They were the three words that brought everyone around this couple from rage and disbelief to peace and acceptance.

Sometimes it's just a touch, full of compassion, full of love, uncorrupted by the games people play, uncompromised by ego that usually runs people's lives.

Some of you have your own experiences of what it is like to be in a room with a person who never attempts to manipulate you. Who has no interest in lecturing you or impressing you or converting you to something or someone you are not. Who considers you perfect and totally acceptable exactly the way you are.

Every time I put pressure on myself to be a better mom, to help Lina more, to be more efficient, more tuned in, I have to stop and realize that this is my own little game I am playing with myself. Lina has never asked me to change a single thing about myself. She has always let me be exactly who and where I am. She doesn't respond to anything fake. She doesn't let herself be controlled by anything other than love and compassion. She loves a lot of people, and her love is pure. She wants foot rubs and back rubs and music and reading out loud from books. She wants to swing in her hammock and go for long walks and even longer car rides. She wants to jump on trampolines and go to New York City street fairs in the summer. She wants to go to the beach and talk to the ocean. She wants to have as many celebrations as possible with "yellow cake" and "gingersshnap-cookies" and lots of people around. She wants to be included in conversations and respected as a person who understands everything and does not want to be talked about in the third person. She wants to learn and grow and find as many ways as possible to express herself and her own humanity. She is not a trooper, not a hero, not better or worse than anyone else. She is not a teacher, but she teaches. She just is.

One way of understanding where someone is in the energetic world, in terms of frequency and connectedness, is to look at how he or she affects the people and things around them. Call me crazy, but even the plants like Lina's company better than anyone else's. The plants in Lina's room are always greener, fuller, and grow faster. It's the same with people. For someone as socially awkward as Lina, and as intense and truly challenging it can be to ride with her through her rough moments, hours, days, and weeks, she has more people around her with a profound love and appreciation for her than most other people I know.

Almost all of our caretakers (and the term caretaker, by the way, doesn't explain what they do with Lina, or anything about their relationship with her) keep coming back to us and stay in touch long after their lives, their careers, their marriages, their families have taken them away from the day-to-day experience with Lina. Strangers who have met Lina at Atlas, the New York City school Lina was enrolled in for years, still contact me or Tony to tell their own stories about how their meetings with Lina touched them, moved them, enlightened them, uplifted them. Their meeting with Lina took place beyond our regular language. It wasn't inspired by rational thinking. It was about a different frequency from the one we are used to, deep awareness, compassion, and love. For whoever listened closely, Lina would talk about their auras, their current color that she saw without any effort around any given person.

Everyone around Lina considers themselves to have a special relationship with her. Now I think this is partly something we project onto kids with special needs, our special relationship that we have with these special kids. We want to be healers, and we want to be loved by someone who we know isn't capable of lying, like babies, dogs, and, yes, many special needs kids. It used to irritate me when people would come up to me and claim their uniquely important position in Lina's life. I thought about it as self-importance, hero-complex, and ego. But as it kept happening, my feelings of irritation turned into amusement and fascination. How does she do that? How does she make all these people, everyone she is in close contact with, myself included, feel that they are so incredibly special? Tony and Elsa have the same experience! Donovan, our endlessly patient, soft-spoken, deeply empathetic current caretaker, feels it, too. And he is right! No one is making it up. Lina has always had a knack for surrounding herself with very special, uniquely loving, compassionate, and intuitive people. Lina's many friends' and caretakers' understanding of their special relationship with her is absolutely true. They are unique to her. She has the capacity and the connectedness to have unique and extremely meaningful relationships with an endless number of people. Her relationships are not bogged down by ego and complicated back-and-forth manipulations. She can hold so many people in her heart, fully and alive, over time and space. Everyone in Lina's life is the chosen one. It's a wonderful feeling to be held in someone's heart in that way. The closer Lina gets to her own healing, beyond the physical and emotional discomfort of her conditions, disorders, whatever you want to call them, the more I remember her as a little girl, before autism.

So many people, healers—shamans, teachers, friends, babysitters, therapists, herbalists, homeopaths, sound therapists, NeuroMovement practitioners, alternative health care professionals—have been involved in Lina's treatments.

Like vaccines, autism too has become an industry. Endless types of professionals profit from this epidemic. Parents get themselves into debt that they struggle for the rest of their lives to get out of, just to try that one additional treatment that looks so promising and has had such a powerful positive impact on so many kids who look just like their own. The situation, for so many families, is so dire and desperate that parents will do almost anything, pay with money they don't have, travel all around the Earth, listen to any healing professional with an open heart, make themselves small, make themselves big, make themselves into anything that will help them find their way back to their children. Undoubtedly, wherever there is potential profit to be made, there is exploitation. Unreasonable fees. Ruthless charges. Impossible cancellation policies. But not everyone is like that. Some practitioners, some healers, are simply interested in helping those who suffer. They just want to make a difference. See someone being brought back to comfort, well-being, peace, and joy.

One such individual is Scott P. Huber. While I was in the process of looking into treatments for Lina's mycoplasma infection, a friend of mine whom I met when studying NeuroMovement with Anat Baniel told me about Scott. He does acupressure allergy and sensitivity treatments, she told me, and has helped many children with autism over the years. Scott refers to himself as an alternative health care practitioner and works with bioenergetic allergy elimination techniques and applied kinesiology. Muscle testing is an important part of these techniques, Scott explains, because it offers a quick and easy way to determine a person's potential sensitivity to a substance. This helps not only with things such as foods, inhalants, and contactants, but can also be helpful when attempting to decide which supplements and treatments will benefit a person. From the very beginning, Scott was very careful to point out that his work, like that of most others, is a gradual process and not at all a quick fix. He is supportive of a wide range of treatments and never claims to have all the answers. Scott works with vials and saliva and tapping on the spine and lives in a world where energy, love, intuition, focus, and integrity are what heals people. The first time Lina and Roshelle and I drove up the hill to his modest house in Warren, the little New Jersey town an hour and a half away from New York City, I had no idea what to expect. As we walked into the waiting room, Lina reluctantly following along, his wife greeted us cheerfully by the reception desk. Lina grabbed a magazine from the rack on the wall and sat down, crossed her legs, and started to speed-turn the pages through the magazine. But when it was time to walk through the glass doors of Scott's office, Lina had no trouble transitioning. She walked right in, magazine in hand, and sat down on the rolling chair next to Scott's desk. Scott, a large, friendly man with a huge mustache and a teddy-bear kind of calm, gentle presence, smiled and started to take out vials from the hundreds of tiny drawers behind his desk. There was a vial for mycoplasma, one for hormones, one for gluten, one for MMR, one for the immune system, one for Epstein-Barr virus, and many more. As I described what Lina's challenges were, Scott picked out the relevant vials and muscle-tested Lina for their impact on her through me. Lina held onto the vial. I had my hand on Lina's shoulder. Scott then asked me to hold out my other arm and resist his pushing it down. This is called surrogate muscle testing. As the mycoplasma bottle was in the stand, my arm was pushed down easily. When he was done testing all the different vials, he asked Lina if she would let him tap along her spine as she held onto the vials that had tested positive. Lina agreed, and as Scott was done, he retested her, again through me.

"Better," Scott commented half to himself, half to me and Lina, and went on to tap some more along Lina's spine.

During the next "arm test" my arm stayed up, and Scott concluded that Lina was done for the day. This procedure became our weekly Tuesday afternoon routine. Roshelle and I would pick up Lina early from school and drive out to Scott's office. I began to count on the smiles and well-being that Lina emanated after these visits. She was clearly in a much better space, particularly the first couple of days after the sessions. Calmer, happier, less obsessive, and less anxious. A few months into the treatment, I decided to try it, too.

"So," Scott asked me when it was my turn, "what would you like to have help with?"

"Well, I don't want to tell you all kinds of stories that are just going to reinforce the wrong things, but I guess I feel like there is more going out than coming in. . . . I know that ultimately, that's not really true, but I am tired; it's been a rough ride."

As Roshelle drove us home, I fell asleep in Lina's lap. That had never happened before. After a few of my own sessions, I began to notice a more consistent sense of well-being. Less fear. More joy. More calm. I slept better. I felt that I didn't have to work quite as hard to attain a sense of everything being ok. Lina seemed to have similar experiences. Moments of peace, away from her obsessions, grew longer. And her OCD caused her less anxiety.

One time, though, as we pulled into Scott's driveway, Lina wasn't as willing to leave the car as usual. And she didn't run into his office as willingly as she had for most of the treatment. Scott had to work through me, tapping on my spine as I held my hand on Lina's shoulder.

On our way back to the city after this visit, Lina was unusually quiet. At some point, as we were approaching the Lincoln Tunnel, I looked over at Lina and noticed her face being partly flushed and partly without any color at all. As I looked closer, I noticed Lina had red blotches all over her body. Her eyes were glazed, and her hands were hot and sweaty. She seemed out of it and reminded me of how she used to look right before her seizures. I took off her thick sweater, her shoes, and her socks and asked Roshelle, who was driving, to turn on cold air.

"Oh my God," Roshelle gasped as she caught a glance of Lina in the back mirror, "should I get off the next exit?"

"No, just keep driving, this is in the middle of nowhere. I'm going to call Scott."

Scott didn't seem intimidated by Lina's dramatic change.

"It's just her detoxing, I'm going to work on her over the phone. You'll see her looking better soon."

It was another minute with Scott on the phone, and Lina's color returned to normal; the blotches all over her body disappeared; her body temperature dropped, and she seemed instantly ok.

"Wow," I joked with Roshelle later, "This is a whole new level of hocus-pocus!"

We drove to Lina's school, and I walked her up and settled next to her in the hammock in the sensory gym. Lina was quiet and didn't want to eat her lunch.

"Lina, do you want to go home instead, and rest, and come back here tomorrow?" I asked her.

"Go home."

"Okay baby, let's go home."

Lina relaxed at home for the rest of the day. In the late afternoon, she threw up. In the evening, her smiles and affectionate gestures, the way she looked at me with so much love and awareness, reminded me of her toddler years. I thought to myself, it's really happening, we are going to get Lina back; the day when all her challenges and discomforts are over is coming closer.

We went regularly, every Tuesday, and I could see how Lina felt great the night and the first couple of days after our visit, and then gradually, the benefits would wear off until the next visit, when her sense of well-being, presence, and calm would peak again. For as long as that was true, I would come pick Lina up early every Tuesday to beat the traffic and drive the hour-and-a-half ride to Scott's little house up on the hill. Lina, who almost always has trouble transitioning out of her beloved "blue car," would make her regular exception for Scott. She would get out of the car without hesitating, march straight into the waiting room, and, without pause, proceed into his office. One such time, after her treatment, I told Lina what I always told her:

"Okay, love, it's my turn, go take a walk with Roshelle outside and I'll meet you in the car in a little while."

Normally Lina would have left to take her walk, but this time she walked back to the chair she had been sitting in during the treatment.

"No," she said, with determination. "My head."

I looked at Scott.

"Did you do the neurotransmitters today?" I asked him.

"No, let's do that, and the brain."

Lina smiled and held onto me as Scott tapped along her spine while she held onto the little neurotransmitters and brain vials.

"You are telling us what we forgot. That's pretty cool, Lina," I said and smiled back at my uncanny daughter. When it was done, I again encouraged Lina to go find Roshelle in the waiting room, but Lina, who was beginning to get a hang of how this was going to get better, said:

"Feet! Belly and feet!" and again sat down in the treatment chair, smiling as Scott and I eventually figured she was asking for help to get grounded and also to negate the effects of Wi-Fi, the EMF (Electro Magnetic Frequency), as well as with balancing good and bad bacteria in her gut. I looked at my beautiful, intelligent, unusually connected and aware teenager, thirteen years old at the time, and wondered what it must be like to know so much more than the average person and yet have access to such a limited repertoire of words to describe it.

CHAPTER FIVE

The Ongoing Search for Healing and Peace

W HAT HEALS US? As a psychotherapist, I have asked myself that question many times over the decades of working with people who are actively seeking healing for their agony, fear, depression, ambivalence, addictions, creativity blocks, PTSD, whatever it may be. And I do believe that there is a lot of healing in relationships. I do think that some of us chose to be healers in some way because we trust that we can help others and make a real difference in someone's life. That our hearts can beat, not just for ourselves, but for someone else, too. Being a mother to a teenage girl who oscillates between hope and despair, feeling good and feeling terrible, my motivation to find the answer to that question amplified enormously. And, I found, healing is not just about finding the right people to help Lina. It's not just the right food, the right diet, the right supplement and the right herbs, the most effective probiotic, the purest fish oil, the right homeopathic drops, the most effective therapies. One of Lina's healers is the ocean.

When we couldn't go to Sweden, we chose another place, a closer place that also had the ocean. Our Fire Island trip was the scariest week of our lives. But Tony and I both know that the ocean is still one of Lina's most powerful healers. In spite of our near-drowning experience, Lina kept talking about "the yellow bathing suit to the ocean." By the end of that summer, Tony and I would have both either laughed or cried about the prospect of taking another trip with Lina, particularly if it involved a plane ride. I guess you could say we both heal fast and both have a tendency to get hopeful again pretty quickly. Accordingly, the day after Christmas, only six months after Lina's mycoplasma infection diagnosis, Tony, Lina, Elsa, Roshelle, and I were on a 6 a.m. flight to Miami Beach. During the flight, Lina sat in her chair, smiling at me and leaning forward to distribute a kiss on my forehead or hand every couple of minutes in that way that always makes me briefly wonder, "Do I really want to change anything about her?" We were all in the turquoise ocean waves before noon. Lina obsessed about yellow cookies, pink watermelon, taxi rides, and "blue car with mom" all the way up to the hotel room, through the elevator ride down to the poolside, through the walk on the boardwalk, through the sand, all the way down to the water's edge. But the moment her feet touched the ocean water, her obsessions subsided. A soft, introverted smile spread on her beautiful face, her movements went from jerky and disorganized to smooth and well coordinated, leisurely and harmonious. I never cease to be amazed at the impact that the ocean has on her.

One day, Lina again obsessed about pineapple and pink watermelon. She'd seen the fruit on trays near the pool. This time, her OCD escalated, and she started to yell. "PINK WATERMELON! CAN I PLEAAASE HAVE SOME PINK WATERMELON!" and threw herself on the ground. The modified Atkins diet, allowing only 15–20 carbohydrates a day but as many calories as anyone can pack in through meats, oils, and carb-less green leafy vegetables, is very effective in treating severe inflammation, yeast, and seizure disorders. However, it doesn't allow for any fruit. So, it was painful for Lina to see all those juicy "pink" pieces of watermelon and not be able to have any. Tony and I walked her toward the beach to get away from people without having to hide in the hotel room. Lina lay down in the sand, screaming about the fruit that she felt so deprived of in that moment. She foamed at the mouth, and I was wondering if this episode was going to degenerate to past proportions where we had to hold her down in order to stop her from punching and biting herself or us. It didn't. But it wasn't going away anytime soon. Tony took her hand and half dragged, half cajoled her through the sand into the water. The moment her body was covered in water, that smile spread across Lina's face. The ocean, like so many times before, saved her. It reminded her in a wordless way, without trying to alter or convince or change her, that she was free and happy again, no matter what her brain was telling her.

Even from a scientific point of view, the ocean, as well as direct contact with the ground, heals. Stephanie Seneff, senior research scientist at the Computer Science and Artificial Intelligence Laboratory of the Massachusetts Institute of Technology, argues that one of the most important problems in autism is sulfate deficiency in the cerebrospinal fluid. This deficiency messes up the generating of new neurons. The lack of sulfate in cerebrospinal fluid, according to Seneff, comes about because of glyphosate (Roundup). It is "a train wreck" for sulfate homeostasis, Seneff argues, and not only disrupts the production of sulfate in the brain that is responsible for regenerating neurons, but also leads to poor protection of the brain. The remedy, in Seneff's view, is sunlight, ocean water, and walking barefoot on the ground, which not only provides the Vitamin D that communicates to a system that everything is ok, but also produces the cholesterol sulfate that's deficient in so many kids with autism.

North Salem is still our second home. When we first moved in, the deer in the area seemed to believe it was their primary residence. They were everywhere, ten, fifteen of them at a time out on the big, hilly field in front of the house. We had a large pumpkin sitting on the stone wall in front of the house. One December afternoon, as Lina, Elsa, Roshelle, and I drove up to the house, an unusually substantial deer was standing in front, eating the pumpkin. Whether the pumpkin had been rolled off the wall by the wind or assisted by the deer, I don't know, but in the fall, it had split open, and the large animal was happily feasting on pumpkin meat and seeds. As the deer spotted us, it reluctantly trotted off to our neighbor's land. I love the sight of these graceful animals around the house. But ticks and Lyme disease are a huge problem in this part of the country, and deer are a primary host for ticks. I imagined a fence all around the five-and-a-half acres, to keep the deer out and rein in a future dog, maybe even a horse one day, and chickens and goats. So one weekend, Marvin—Lina's gym coach and personal friend, a former gymnast and circus artist who wanted to be involved in the transformation of our North Salem home—and I built a fence for a fifteen-by-twenty-five-foot garden just outside the kitchen. Next, we dug post holes all around the field. For most holes, we simply used a post-hole digging shovel and what we started to refer to as "the negotiator," a heavy-duty digging bar known for making its way through the ground with a determination that the shovel cannot always manage.

As I walked across the field, with a bunch of wooden poles, pulling the shovel and "the negotiator" with me on the little green cart I got at Home Depot, my home away from home these early days of setting up our North Salem life, I could almost hear the kids' laughter as they ran after each other up and down the little hills or jumped into the pool on a hot summer day, after having chased away the goats from the little fenced-in area around the pool. In my mind's eye, I saw Lina reluctantly leaving her cozy, warm bed before dawn to walk with me over to the chicken coop to collect the eggs that we would have for breakfast. Those happy visions helped me explain to myself why I found myself working less and less within my professional field, as a psychotherapist and, as of recently, a NeuroMovement practitioner, and spending more and more time up in the North Salem house, dragging the green wagon full of poles, digging two-foot-deep holes, preparing for change, preparing to help Lina get the healing benefits of trees, soil, grass, and an open sky that shows stars at night that are barely visible in the city sky.

This was my way to take the results of Seniff's research and provide Lina with the natural Vitamin D that would produce the cholesterol sulfate that she lacks. Walking barefoot on this soil would reduce inflammation in Lina's system. Getting North Salem was Tony's and my way of listening to Malidoma's wise words about Lina's need for allies in nature, trees, birds, flowers, and an open sky that would reassure her that she can keep her connectedness with multiple frequencies, with her internal magical, beautiful, colorful world, while at the same time finding a way to communicate and exist in more harmonious ways in our world. Getting this farm was an attempt to listen to my own internal wisdom of what Lina needed. And what Elsa and I needed, too. And if it worked out in the way I imagined for us, I would extend the benefits of this land to others. Maybe other kids like Lina. Maybe all kinds of kids and maybe their parents, too. Or maybe just some friends of Lina and Elsa. Whoever showed up in our lives.

Those were the thoughts that flowed through my head as I dug yet another hole in the ground, stuck the post in, and packed the soil all around it. Someone suggested cutting the roots that were in the way of the hole digging. The idea bewildered me. I am grateful for every tree that grows all around the fields. Cutting through the roots of one those trees seems as absurd as trying to flatten out the hilly land or cursing at the sun for warming up the frozen ground or trying to manipulate the stars to form a different pattern that would be more pleasing to me. Nature is genius. There is nothing to improve. Nothing to conquer. It is perfect and pleasing beyond my wildest imagination. Cutting the roots of one of those trees whose branches the large white hawk lands on early in the morning was not an option.

It is the way I want to approach people, too. Lina. Her OCD. There is someone inside all those repetitions who desperately wants to be heard. Not just heard, but appreciated. Not just appreciated, but learned from, fully respected. In the middle of all the chaos, in the middle of everything Lina requires from her environment just to make it through the day, she often creates a kind of upside-down magic that I haven't found with anyone else.

It was Monday. Roshelle, our wonderful aid for the past three-and-a-half years, had just told me she would be leaving us. At one point, after Sean, our previous babysitter, left, I was without help for a year. I just couldn't find the right person. Then Roshelle came around, and she, I instantly knew, was the right one. We all love Roshelle, and I might have experienced the news of her leaving as something to be upset about, but I felt it would be okay. I felt that things would work out. I had been out in North Salem with Coach Marvin that day during the kids' school day, to shovel snow from the driveway and plan the continuation of our fence building. We had tried to build up a snow hill using the snow blower, but there wasn't enough snow to throw, so we simply shoveled snow onto a tarp and dragged it over to the top of the hill. It wasn't quite happening, and soon we dropped the snow hill project and instead went to the studio to figure out on which wall the speed bag should be attached. Later that evening, back in the city, Roshelle, the girls, and I decided to have an early dinner and go outside sledding. Halfway to the hill in the park down the street, Lina started to get increasingly upset, looping about "the blue car and yellow mom." I told Roshelle and Elsa to keep going and start sledding while I stayed behind with Lina.

"I get that you really want to go in the blue car with me, my love. I get that."

"Blue car with mom. In the garage."

"You are right, Lina, the car is in the garage. Tomorrow I'm going to go there and get it and pick you up at school so we can drive to Scott Huber. Today we are sledding. Tomorrow we are driving in the blue car."

"Get the blue car in the GARAAAAGE!"

Lina was getting increasingly loud. She was half crying, half screaming.

"Write down BLUUUE CAAAR!" she shrieked.

I hadn't brought the paper and markers that I usually bring to clarify for Lina with sketches, words, and visual schedules what would happen next. Whenever faced with these kinds of anxiety-provoking episodes, where whatever was going to happen was the sheer opposite of what Lina wanted, visual clarifications were a big help.

"Lina, we could go back home and write down blue car and talk about when that will happen or we can go sledding."

"BLUE CAR IN THE GARAGE!" Lina screamed and cried so loudly that the maintenance guys in the nearby building started to move toward us to see what was going on.

I felt peace. It didn't matter to me whether we went sledding or back home.

"Lina, I love you so much. It's not easy, baby, but it's going to pass. Whatever you're feeling right now is going to pass, and you'll be smiling again. What do you think, should we go back home and read and swing in the hammock?"

"Sledding."

By the time we got to the hill, Lina was smiling. She would normally need some convincing to go down, and most of the time she would prefer sitting on the sled with someone. She would like the repetition of the same sled with the same person. This year, the purple sled was the chosen one. This time, however, Lina wanted to go by herself and took off. Elsa excitedly jumped on the green body-surfing board that worked well on the snow and joined Lina. The snow was packed well, and they both had a nice, speedy glide down the hill. As usual, after her ride, Lina just sat at the bottom of the hill, seemingly unsure of what to do next. This is something I noticed soon after her regression, that Lina no longer seemed to know, not only how to tie together sentences, but also how to sequence and tie together consecutive events. Or actually, I think she knew what to do, but not how to execute it, similar to her speech. She understood and had thoughts, but when she tried to express herself, the words came out wrong. So, she would just stand somewhere, waiting for someone to help her get to the next thing. Elsa, intuitively aware of this lack of piecing things together, ran over to Lina and hugged her, praising her for her boldness in going down the hill by herself. Lina enjoyed the feedback of her new-won bravery and smiled softly at Elsa's affection.

"Go to Mom's house," she then requested. I think Lina's constant requesting of the things that she wants to happen next, which is always in opposition to what she has at the moment, is at the core of every obsessive thought. Rather than being a kind of dissatisfaction with what is, I believe it's a way to negotiate anxiety that is so strong and overpowering that it feels fragmenting. And that's why the little visual sketches help Lina to puzzle together again what was dissolved in her mind by the anxiety.

I said, "Sure, let's go," but as we got to the top of the hill, Lina was ready to go down again. This time she wanted to go "with Elsa." Back at the bottom, the two of them just sat there. Lina, because she had trouble with puzzling together the next sequence; Elsa, out of her desire to join and feel connected with Lina. As we walked together up the hill, Lina again requested to "go back home to Mom's house." But back on top, Lina didn't make any gesture to leave the hill. Instead, she requested the "green sled."

"You want to try the snowboard!" I exclaimed enthusiastically, thrilled at this level of bold variation.

"No."

"Okay, not that," I offered, in a more somber tone.

"The green sled," Lina said again, looking over to the side.

I looked where she had glanced, and by a little pine tree was a green-and-yellow sled that someone must have left behind. It had a broken handle, but Lina didn't mind. She wanted to try that one anyway. Elsa, Roshelle, and I were quietly excited at this bold and uncharacteristic wish to switch things up. Lina again wanted to go down the hill by herself. But at the bottom, something amazing happened. She didn't just sit there, waiting for someone to come show her what to do next. She stood up, smiled, and ran up the hill.

"Sled down the hill," she said excitedly. And that wasn't all; she now requested the snowboard. At the bottom, she again rose up and ran up the hill. Next ride was the purple sled. The following time, she was back to the green, broken one. The moon was almost full, and, while the stars are so much more visible out in North Salem, we could all see them as we lay down on our backs in the snow.

You just never know. With Lina. With Life. I tried to build a snow hill out in North Salem, and what really ended up happening was that we had breakthrough sledding on the little hill down our street in the city. I have never, since Lina was three-and-a-half, seen this level of follow-through, running up the hill on her own initiative after a ride; or desire for variation, picking a different sled for each ride. Walking back home that night, I felt the distance between us and the moon and the stars shrinking.

A week later, Elsa, Lina, Roshelle, and I were back up in North Salem. We were sledding down the little hill at the far end of the field in front of the house. Lina walked over to the fence, where Marvin had built a little gate that would allow us to get through the neighbor's property and to the lake. Lina had never walked the path to the lake, but it was as if she intuitively knew there was water nearby. She just kept walking down the little path and through a ditch next to a fence that separates our neighbor's land from a country club. She kept on walking through thorny bushes and a little frozen spring until we were standing in front of the lake. Ice and a thin layer of snow covered the lake in most places.

"Can I please walk on quiet snow? Quiet quiet, can I please have some quiet?" she asked with urgency.

Before I was even halfway through my explanation that we just have to stand next to it for now, as we couldn't be sure it would hold us, she ran out onto the ice. I carefully and as quickly as I could tiptoed out to where she was and dragged her back to solid ground. A large, beautiful white hawk flew over us and settled on a nearby tree next to the lake, scaring away a bunch of black crows. They made loud, protesting crow sounds but quickly flew out of the way of the hawk.

"Quiet snow quiet snow . . ." She tried to talk me into it. "Mom please quiet snow, my yellow mom, quiet can I please have some quiet I am tired, Helena can I please have some quiet snow . . ."

The urgency in her words moved me. I wished I could take her out there. My explanations weren't getting through to her. I wished I could understand her better. I think this may have been the first time Lina had experienced ice on a lake. What did she mean about being tired? Did she want to go and drown? Swim? Just be on the quiet ice? Her earnest request was so deeply moving. I held my hand over my heart.

"Oh, Lina, I feel how much you want this. I so want to understand you. I hear you, my love, you are tired. I know you want to be on the quiet snow. I think I understand how important it is for you right now."

My words, or rather, the feeling behind the words, my urgency matching hers, calmed her down a little. She connected with my understanding of the importance. She took a deep breath. She looked at me. Then we walked back through the thorns and the ditch and the little path, to our field where Roshelle and Elsa were still "snowboarding" down the hill.

One Sunday afternoon, before we had to pack up and go back to the city, I had the idea to bring Lina with me outside to count up the fence poles that were almost all in the ground, so I could figure out how many rolls of the deer barrier I needed to order.

"Lina, you and I will get the job done."

"Green chocolate in the car!"

"Yes, okay chocolate in the car after counting poles."

"Greeeeen Chocolate!!!!"

"You got it. First poles, then chocolate."

"IN THE CAAAAAR."

"Yep. Let's see, one two three four . . . eleven, twelve . . ." I was counting as we were slowly walking from one pole to the other, all around the field . . . Lina reluctantly followed along, now and then reminding me about the chocolate and how she wanted it "in the blue car with my yellow mom and with a spoon."

We kept going.

"Tjugo-fyra, tjugo-fem . . ." I always switch from English to Swedish when counting anything more than twenty. I have heard that counting, for a foreigner, is the last thing that stays more accessible in the mother tongue.

By forty, Lina was done. She stopped walking and started screaming. I just kept on counting poles and walking. She screamed louder and didn't move. It was green chocolate, blue car, music, the "Love me do" song (by the Beatles), seat belt on, etc., etc. It was everything but counting more poles. I had in my head that somehow, we had to get through counting before we could go back, and my inflexibility about it made Lina's objection ten times worse. She eventually sat down in a wet, muddy field, refusing to move, bitterly complaining about the lack of green chocolate in her life.

"Well, we are having it now. Here. It's not always the same. Today we are eating it here in this muddy field!" I told her, not without irritation in my voice.

"Greeen chocolate!!! In the car!! Put the seat belt on!"

"There is no such thing as green chocolate! Why do you always want something other than what you're having right now?! You miss your whole life doing that, always wishing for something other than what is!" I lectured her; me, too, feeling miserable about the misery she was feeling and making up all kinds of stories in my head about how everything was a struggle and nothing was easy, not even counting a bunch of poles in a beautiful field as the late winter sun was melting frozen ground into mud.

"Can I please have Roshelle!" she responded and added, "I want my Elsa please!" And then, as if she had eventually processed my complaints and realized there was some truth to it even though the delivery wasn't flawless, she suddenly smiled, looked at me softly, and said, "Can I please have you."

We sat still in the muddy field for another ten minutes, letting the sun melt away the rest of our sorrows, and then slowly walked back, hand in hand, to the house, the car, and the "green" chocolate.

CHAPTER SIX

More Challenges and More Solutions

ONE OF THE things Lina has taught me is that I have to get better at asking for help. Before Lina's breakdown, I had no intention of having anyone but myself and Tony care for our kids. During this period, getting help is a basic ingredient in getting through the day gracefully. When Roshelle told me that she was leaving, I knew she was doing the right thing. She had been good to us for a long time, and she needed to focus on her own life, her marriage, her education, her next step. I thought it would work out. But I also knew how difficult it had been to find the right person before she just showed up one day and I knew she was the one we had been waiting for.

We already had Donovan, who would pick up Lina a couple of times a week. Eventually, Donovan took over Roshelle's work and is still with us, but at the time, he only had very limited hours to offer. I began my search with a certain desperation. I was so eager for a quick, smooth solution that my sense of urgency clouded my judgment. Quickly, I hired the nephew and the brother of my friend Maria. Both without legal papers, car, language, or knowledge about the area. And so it was that I hired Louis, a person who had never seen snow, help me take care of our North Salem house our first winter. Somehow, the situation had developed from Maria suggesting I just meet her brother and nephew who were coming to the city, without any pressure to hire them, to "Well, they are here now and I think it's only fair that you give them each a month, since they bought their own tickets just to get here."

Juan, according to Maria, was basically Jesus's little brother, capable of doing anything, roll with anything, committed, and 100 percent ready for the challenge of being Lina's aide. Brother Louis had left his kids in Mexico City, his whole life, just to come here to be helpful to us. Maria was talking about organic giving, straight from the heart, the unselfish wishes to be of service to me and my kids at great sacrifice. Somehow, the situation then rapidly escalated to me standing on my own driveway, watching my friend, her nephew, her brother, and another nephew unloading the car with "donations" to the house and the belongings of Juan and Louis. I had a sense of foreboding as I watched my friend fill up the refrigerator with corn tortillas, mayonnaise, hummus, and sourdough bread. I listened in awe as I heard my friend elaborate on her gift to my family over dinner.

I made it clear that there was no agreement and no guarantees for any amount of time and that the only two people that I would ever guarantee anything to at this point in my life were Lina and Elsa.

As my friend expressed surprise about my lack of gratitude for her gifts, including a large seashell that had great personal value to her, I pointed out the glitches in our agreement. I explained how little interest I had in anyone making sacrifices for us, never mind leaving their own children to be with my children. How important honesty was for me and how both Juan and Louis, in my understanding, were simply searching for an opportunity outside of Mexico City. And that it would either work or it wouldn't. I clarified my uncertainty about having someone live with us who didn't have a car or papers, and that I had no idea how her nephew would respond to Lina any more than how she would respond to him. The experience made me doubt my own ability to figure out how to help Lina, to find the right people, or to create the right circumstances, for all three of us. Running around in the store a week later, trying to find the right soup for Maria's brother who didn't have a car, I thought, *how was it possible that I had managed to make things harder for myself? Where was my trust in an easier existence? More effective help?*

On a mild, drizzly Tuesday in early February in the city, a week after Juan started working with Lina, he was going to take her for a walk while I ran out to the market to get dinner. While I was standing in line, waiting to pay, I got a message from Juan that is the nightmare of every parent, especially if you have a child with autism. "I'm on West 69th Street and Amsterdam I lost Lina come fast please she ran and I can't find her this is real."

It took me a few seconds to believe what I'd read, but then I dropped my shopping cart and was outside the store in less than a second. I sprinted the five blocks with every unimaginable thought racing through my mind—with flashbacks of similar sprints when Lina first started running away from us at three-and-a-half; with fear and hope about who would find her, how they would respond to her, how she would respond to them; with disbelief; with rage; with every possible emotion rinsing through my high-alert, adrenaline-busting system. As I got closer, I tried to picture 69th Street, Lina, and where I would go if I were she. Probably to a bakery or a place with lots of fruit, or to a Duane Reade, with shelves full of sugary things . . . I ran the last block, trying to trust that Lina was protected, that everything would be okay, that everything would work out because it always had. When I got to 69th and I saw Lina standing there with a very shaky Juan, having walked back the same way she had run off, I sobbed and held onto her without any intention of ever letting her go again. Later on, my happier, more confident, self argued that nothing serious had happened and that this experience most likely would help prevent something much more serious from occurring. The joy and gratitude of having Lina back intact, smiling, safe, outweighed every other emotion. At first. Lina's escape brought back memories of many such runaways, with me sprinting down streets, running on instinct, hoping and praying that I would catch sight of her unruly blond curls and get to hold her hand safely in mine and walk with her back home. Now I feared my phone's notification chime from the next message from Juan or someone else, dreading that it would be about Lina being gone, out of sight, away from someone capable of protecting her from the unpredictable streets of New York City.

Juan did not know how to cook. He didn't want to learn how to be with Lina. He was overwhelmed by her breakdowns. I cut my losses and drove him to North Salem to have him help his uncle finish up the fence instead. The day after I left him there, he messaged me with an image of the pipes in the ceiling bulging through the paint. Juan had bathed in the antique-looking bathtub, and the water had leaked through the ceiling. The following day, I drove back up with Lina and Roshelle (who was still in the process of winding down her time with us with once-a-week visits) to let Juan and Louis know that our agreement would end after they finished the fence. The night before, Elsa had been crying and described how having Juan around felt lonely. He had never said anything to her and didn't seem to care who she was. Was it Juan's fault that he couldn't cook? Relate? Was it his fault that he lost Lina? Busted the pipes? I don't think it matters. The search continued. Later that night, after the talk with Juan and Louis, Lina was in the bathtub, chatting away about all the things she wanted. Mostly it was foods, ice cream in a blue bowl and chicken with red sauce, but also to put the purple shoes on and go for a walk, and Bob Marley's "Lively Up Yourself" song. It was so quiet. Lina was so present. She asked me to pour warm water on her as she stretched out her long legs in the tub.

"Can I please have more warm water splash."

"You sure can," I agreed and dipped the green plastic bowl in the water and poured it over her.

"More!"

"Ah, do you mean warmer?"

"Warmer, warm water splash."

Roshelle stuck her head through the bathroom door. I decided to let Lina stay by herself in the shallow bathtub water while I quickly brought Roshelle with me to check on a carpentry job that was done from underneath the kitchen floor. Back upstairs, Lina, still in the bathtub, was not happy with me.

"This is no joke!" she said with a sharp, loud voice.

It took her a good twenty minutes to calm down after having felt abandoned in the bathtub. Later that night, I told her how much I appreciated her letting me know how she felt and that I realized being left like that did not feel good or funny to her. She smiled, transmitting that warm glow that only Lina can. What a huge leap forward that was for her to describe her feelings in that clear and direct way. How fundamental it is to us humans to express ourselves and to be understood.

We were in our last stretch with Roshelle. Lina and Elsa both had a day off from school, so the four of us went to IKEA. We were buying a bed for Elsa's room in North Salem and two armchairs, one for Elsa's room and one for mine. Lina walked with her arm in mine, putting up with the harsh fluorescent light and the unexpected crowds the best she could, obsessing intermittently about yellow cookies and the blue car.

"So, how do I get something delivered?" I asked one of the IKEA workers.

"You can have someone help you get your items to the delivery department, it would cost you $40, or you can pick up your items yourself and take it through the cashier and bring it to the delivery section yourself."

I turned to Roshelle, "Who wouldn't pick up their own items? What's the big deal, putting it on a cart, wheeling it down the aisle; how hard can it be?"

"I know you wouldn't!" Roshelle laughed.

She was right. I wouldn't. Why ask someone else to do something that I am perfectly capable of doing myself? And also, in some way, Lina is sometimes an extra incentive for me to do things myself. I don't want to use her as an excuse for things. I want to try to live as a free person, knowing that if I do, Lina and Elsa will benefit. I want to try to get through difficult situations now and then so I know that we can. I don't want to allow autism to make us smaller. I am hoping it can make us bigger, larger, freer, more compassionate, bolder, more trusting. Having said all that, as I was piling up all the boxes on the cart and trying to maneuver the whole mound through the checkout line, I was beginning to comprehend why there was an option to pay $40 for someone else to do it. Waiting further in the line to the delivery desk, the choice to dish out $40 dollars did seem increasingly appealing, particularly since Lina's tolerance for neon lights, people, and energetic shopping frustration all around her was running lower. Her voice was becoming louder, more shrill.

"Can I please have the blue car and drive with music!"

"You sure will! Just finishing up, then we're out of here! You want to sit down over there on that couch while you wait?"

"NO!"

She started wringing her hands and wiggling her pelvis in that unsettling way, where she is actually slightly dislocating her femur bones from the pelvis bone in her desperate search for calming sensory input and relief from tension. I was just getting ready to step in but stopped as I watched Elsa get Lina to hop up on an empty cart and then push her across the hall, jump on the cart, and slide with Lina over the smooth stone floor. They took turns, Lina reluctantly pushing Elsa, who was supporting her through successful navigation across the floor in the opposite direction. They began to flow together, the way only Lina and Elsa can. Through love and intelligence, Elsa helped her older sister cope with the harsh sensory conditions and discover the possibilities of an empty cart and a smooth floor in a spacious store.

There is no one like Elsa. She dances her way through life, spreading her love and sense of adventure all around her. She is cool and free, patient and warm. She gives and gives and keeps getting richer. She is wild and silly and whimsical; her room is a mess. She looks at people and life with surprising clarity. She loves imperfection; she finds it heartwarming and reassuring rather than irritating and in need of fixing. I take a deep breath, there on the delivery line at IKEA, watching my two girls find a way to turn waiting into a cart race.

There are days with flow and days with challenges. With Lina, I never know what is going to happen. I try to not make anyone else, including Lina, responsible for my happiness. It's not always easy.

Lina came home one day after school and wanted to go right back out. Normally we walk home from 29th Street and 8th Avenue, where Lina's school is, all along the Hudson River to my apartment forty-five blocks away. But today Roshelle had picked Lina up from school, and then they'd taken an Uber car back. So, when Lina wanted to go back outside, I turned the oven with the roasted chicken and cauliflower off and said, "Let's go!" Elsa needed to get some presents for upcoming birthday parties, so I figured I'd take them all to Flying Tigers, a Danish store with every kind of whimsical gadget one can imagine, perfect for twelve-year-old friends, perfect to take Lina to, since this was not a food store and had no candy or baked goods in it. We all walked happily over there, and Lina eventually engaged with all the little toys.

Everything went well until we were walking home. Lina seemed to have misunderstood the situation. She had somehow thought the presents were to be given to Elsa's friends right after the purchase. She had thought there was going to be a party. With yellow cake. With cookies. And wild animals. Elsa had mentioned something about going to the Bronx Zoo for one of the birthday parties, and now, in Lina's mind, a party was approaching, with cake, a blue car ride, and good friends. My heart sank as I saw my Lina getting increasingly disorganized by the disappointment of no party, no cake, no car ride, no wild animals, and no friends. She began to pop her femur bone in and out of her hip joint, and her voice went straight up to a falsetto shriek. The two choices, going back home or going to swing on the tire swing in the Diana Ross playground, were of little comfort to her. We managed to proceed one block closer to home before everything disintegrated. Lina's jab (she should have been the boxer, not me: she has real talent) landed straight between my jaw and my nose, but I registered only a vague sense of pain, caught up with the requirement of the situation, and focused on keeping my disoriented girl safe and everyone around her safely away from her. I had already sent Elsa back home and instructed Roshelle to keep passersby informed of the situation. After Lina's jab, I had quickly found my way behind her, constraining her from any more hitting of herself or me. But Lina is strong. And with the adrenaline shooting through her system while only sadness and concentration was in mine, she managed to wrestle her way out of my arms a couple of times before I had her safely on her back on the ground. Roshelle knew the drill. She took her jacket off and slid it in under Lina's head to avoid any head trauma. As in a bad dream, blurry and surreal, I heard people voicing their urgent comments about what I was doing. I heard dogs growling and now and then caught a glimpse of someone on the phone, perhaps calling 911.

I watched Lina's distorted, distressed face, white foam dripping out of the sides of her mouth.

An agitated policeman stuck his red face into my view.

"Give me some space," he told Roshelle with an impatient voice. I braced myself. When in doubt, don't try to argue with a policeman. Do your thing and keep your voice quiet, I reminded myself.

"What's going on here?" the officer demanded, as he looked at me still holding Lina down on the ground. I was trying to talk to her softly, now and then testing the possibility of being able to gently run my hand through her hair to try to calm her down, while at the same time wary of the possibility of another fist in my face.

"Do you know of anyone with autism?" I asked the policeman with a soft voice.

"Yes," he said, looking away as if going back to the memory of his prior autism experience, "but people have been complaining and calling 911. It's right on the street here, not good!" he lectured, looking like he was somehow stuck between his autism memory and his wish to resolve the disorderly conduct and make use of his badge as quickly as possible.

"I understand. It will pass. This happens about once or twice a month. There is very little I can do but just wait it out."

The policeman mumbled something about how it was in the middle of everyone's way and then disappeared out of my view. Eventually, Lina was calm enough to stand up and reluctantly, not without a lot of residual disappointment and tears, walk back home.

I try not to let these experiences reverberate. I reach for something else. A lighter feeling, a little joke, a brighter thought than the ones circling around the memories of all the coldness, all the helpless fear, the growling dogs, the irritated policemen, the lack of humanity that we are sometimes faced with when a kid with autism falls apart out on public streets. I find relief in the image of strong arms around me, a soft voice from a calm male whispering that everything is going to be okay, Lina will be okay, and a promise, from someone, anyone, that there will be a day when the only thing that's left from those situations are softly fading memories.

As I spent most of the rest of that evening in silence within myself, withdrawn from a world that somehow kept on moving, in spite of what just took place, I thought of something that our new aide, Donovan—who was initially hired not only because of his wonderful caretaking qualities but also because he was a man, big and strong enough to walk Lina safely home from school by himself—recently had mentioned in one of his progress notes. Lina and Donovan had just been leaving Atlas and were about to begin their walk uptown when Lina, faithful to tradition, asked for her "yellow mom." She kept asking, and Donovan kept trying to explain that she would see me the next day, since she was going to Papa's house that afternoon. Lina somehow settled down, realizing, maybe through Donovan's calm demeanor or maybe through some insight of her own, that it simply wasn't going to change, and it was what it was. Then she said, as if partly to herself, partly to Donovan, and partly to the universe:

"Thank you, Mom. God bless you."

I thought about those simple words that whole, long evening after the street incident. And I reminded myself of that when I woke up in the middle of the night after nightmares about blood and catastrophe. And I thought about it every time I felt afraid that my power, my strength, my peace, my joy wouldn't last. And I send it back to Lina. "Thank you, Lina. God bless you." And I thought about the funny situation that happened when Donovan was attempting to show Juan the routine of picking Lina up from school and walk her home. They were with Lina downtown, on the street outside of Atlas, and they intended to walk with her back from school. Lina, as almost always, had her desires set on catching an Uber car instead.

"Save me!" she had shouted, using everything she knows about social situations and social pressure to make her preferred mode of transportation feasible. I thought about this situation and so many other funny, upside-down moments with Lina and how interesting it is to have her in my life, never knowing what she will or won't say and do next. Donovan, as steady and calm as he is, eventually guided Lina back to the original plan, which was to walk along the river back home rather than taking an Uber.

As I reflected on situations like this, I thought about what an awesome honor it is to be constantly challenged to find happiness and peace regardless of what happens, independent of circumstances, moving, step by step, a little closer to the freedom that I know is there for all of us, whenever we are ready to welcome it.

In the spring of 2017, a year after the dramatic onset of the acute mycoplasma infection, Lina's obsessive loops became softer, fewer, and more quickly resolving. Her anxiety was subsiding, as was the whole cycle of obsessive thinking, endless repetitions, jerky movement, screaming, throwing, hitting, and biting. If it weren't for writing this book, I could probably no longer remember when her last serious breakdown had taken place. Lina began smiling through her days and became increasingly flexible; mostly okay with us sometimes taking the car, sometimes the bus, sometimes the subway after our walks halfway home. And when Lina got an hour or two of less walking some of the days, she was still able to fall asleep at a relatively reasonable hour. Her language kept developing. She seemed more at ease in a lot of situations. She accepted her modified Atkin's diet like a champ.

It's not always obvious how to move from crisis to resolution. We often keep fighting battles that have been part of our lives for much longer than is necessary. We act as if the urgency and our adrenaline were still needed, as if the war against whatever we were fighting were still raging. Sometimes we need an outside person to simply remind us that the war is over. Barbara Wosinski, the amazing energy worker, consulted with me about the possibility of Lina participating in a cord-blood transplant research study at Duke University targeted at kids on the spectrum. She focused in on Lina's energy and emotions as we spoke about how we would prepare Lina to receive someone else's blood. We never actually did this procedure, but Barbara's advice about how to do it, if we were to go ahead with it, was still valuable.

"If you are going to do it," Barbara said, "don't do it because you feel that you have to keep fighting for Lina, saving her. She is already in a good place. Just do it because you would like to do something that may be helpful to her, with less urgency." Then she was done talking about my child with autism and turned to me.

"You are afraid of getting stuck in a relationship where you have to give more than you receive," Barbara told me. "You have been giving more and receiving less for your whole life, and you are afraid that you are never going to get your fair share."

"Um, really?"

"Really. And since Lina regressed into autism, you are afraid that she isn't going to get her fair share, either. But that's your worry, not hers. Lina is like, 'What? No!' She is very happy! In fact, she is happier than most kids I have worked on. Most kids lose that kind of freedom and happiness around three or four years old, but Lina still has it. She has so much joy in her belly. She feels loved. She feels accepted. She has everything that she needs. She gets an A+! You get a C-," Barbara added slyly.

I laughed at Barbara's fierce style of putting me in my place. If the message was "Your kid is happy, get over your crusade to save her," then I was happy to be wrong. I felt a sense of calm as Barbara's words slowly sank into my conscience. It was time to stop fighting. It was time to celebrate.

CHAPTER SEVEN

The Lina Effect

Know this: When you say "I,"
the true meaning of "I" is joy, is happiness, it is life,
and it is also the witnessing of life.
Enjoy what comes,
but don't worry about anything at all.
Just be happy, happy, happy.
Know that whatever happens in life, the final point is that
everything is fine.
All is fine.

—MOOJI (JAMAICAN SPIRITUAL LEADER)

There are so many things that make Lina smile. Food. Car rides. Hikes. People. All kinds of people. The nuts, the bus, the driving in the blue car, the people. Lina talks a lot about the people she loves.

"You love so many people, Lina," I commented one evening as Lina was lounging in the bathtub, recounting the people in her life. "Who else do you love?"

"Amanda."

"Yes, you do love Amanda."

"Alison."

"I know that."

"Kirsten. Kristin. Alex. Sidney."

"You love so many."

"Including Sidney."

"Definitely including Sidney."

Lina doesn't seem to get all tangled up in complicated wonderings about what other people do and why. She lives in the world where some blueberries in the forest or swinging in a hammock to Bob Marley's "Lively Up Yourself" seem to be much more important than a million dollars. She spends most of her time in a space that most people struggle to find. When we bend over backward to find Lina, we struggle to find the best part of ourselves. If and when we do find that part of ourselves that just is, that doesn't hold grudges, that doesn't have complicated expectations of others, that doesn't manipulate or threaten, she is already there waiting for us. That's what makes Lina so irresistible. Even when she is mad, she is wholehearted and present about it. And when she is over it, it's like it never happened. And her smile is as new as the sun that rises each morning. She just starts fresh. There may be another loop, sure, but when she is past it, it's gone.

Lina is drawn to pure positive energy. It never fails. She finds it in everyone she meets. A boy in her class at Atlas, whom I'll call Mauro, had spent a lot of time screaming and hitting and struggling to find his own equilibrium. Like Lina, he was very sensitive to energies in other people. If the energy wasn't right, he often felt compelled to strike out.

One morning, Lina leisurely sat down by the long, oval-shaped table in the lunchroom, one of her legs crossed in that almost dainty, nonchalant way that only Lina has, starting in on her four eggs and buttered piece of scone. Mauro came into the lunchroom, yelling loudly. Until he caught a glimpse of Lina. The moment he saw her sitting there, absorbed in her breakfast, he quieted down and sat down in a chair in the corner of the room, watching her every move, smiling. I looked at Alex, one of Lina's main teachers at Atlas, interested in this sudden shift and obvious adoration in Mauro.

"Oh, yeah, we call it the Lina effect," Alex explained later. "It doesn't matter what's going on with Mauro, or how upset he is, as soon as Lina comes into a room, he settles down. He would never sit on the floor during circle time or in the lunchroom or join the group for movie time. But if Lina was in the room, he would watch the whole movie. Before, he wouldn't participate in any of the group activities," Alex explained, "but all that changed with Lina. She is always so balanced these days. Her tone and her calm demeanor really help him, and everyone else in the classroom, too. He used to pull her hair like he would pull all the other kids' hair. But he stopped. Now he just tries to pet her hair and touch her face, and the other day he tried to kiss her. She changed his behavior around. He always leaves before Lina, but the other day she left before him. He had a complete meltdown after she left. He has mellowed out so much for the last couple of months, and I think it's an attribute to his feelings for Lina. As long as he gets to sit and glance over at her, he is ok. He just needs his Lina fix."

I understand him. I need my Lina fix, too. There is something about being with Lina that enhances my understanding of what's important in this life. It's not about finding the perfect words. It's beyond what anyone can say. It's in the being together, seeing each other without explaining anything. It's in the silence—beyond our words, beyond our statements, declarations, aspirations—that stillness and oneness, where love and clarity live. I look into Lina's eyes, and I cannot explain what I see. I walk with her down the street to catch the bus on the way home from school, and the best way I can describe it is that I feel so close to myself, so true to myself, so happy to be human and alive, without thinking about why, without having to justify it. I am home. I am close to who I came into this life to be when I am with her. She knows everything and nothing. Whenever we have our basic needs met, many of us struggle to get to where she is. We meditate, we do yoga, we search for our true self. We try to listen to our inner being, but most of the time we fail because our defensive, justifying, discouraging, analytic, explanatory, entangled, entitled, narcissistic mind chatter is a thousand times louder. And it brings us oceans and mountains away from who we wanted to be when we chose to come into this beautiful and very physical, ever-evolving reality. How ironic that, somehow, we think that we have to save a person like Lina. She doesn't need saving. She doesn't even need acknowledging. She

just is who she is, authentic and real, straightforward and connected deeply to herself as well as to everyone around her.

And she is sensitive. Oh, so sensitive. With her around, it's a
little bit like having a mirror held up to one's own connection
with oneself. When I am close to my inner source, respectful
and loving with myself, harmonious and happy, I know how to
be with Lina. When I am disconnected, caught up in my own
internal dialogue and wrapped up in things that I cannot do
anything about in the moment, I have no idea, no good impulses,
no good strategy on how to relate to her. It simply isn't fun to be
with her while at the same time being disconnected to myself.
She feels it way before I do.

We had a wonderful Saturday night up in North Salem, me
and the girls, my friend Agnes and her kids, and my wonderful
new neighbors, Antwaine and his lovely wife, Tiffany. All of us
sat out on the lawn, eating and talking about life and miracles
and sharing inspiring moments that led to more miracles. Elsa
and Agnes's older daughter, Natalia, were spending time in the
pool. Agnes and I were chasing her little two-year-old Ariana
around the property, talking and laughing. Lina was in the middle of it all, moving back and forth between the hammock that
we put up between two trees and the blanket where everyone
else was sitting, with her sweet energy touching everyone's heart,
smiling, relaxing, enjoying our guests, the food, and the gentle
evening sun. On Sunday morning, Lina's mood suddenly shifted
from happy and cheerful to agitated and restless. No, actually,
let me backtrack. I had someone coming by to fix my stove.
It wasn't going well, and the man was not in a very good mood.
The problem persisted even after the new piece was installed,
so I informed the man that I would pay when the problem

was resolved. The energy got heated, and the man, who somehow wanted to get paid whether the stove was working or not, left reluctantly and in an even worse mood than when he arrived. Lina came into the kitchen and instantly felt the discord. She immediately started to talk about going in the blue car. Lina loves our blue car, but this wasn't about loving the blue car, this was about getting out of an energy field that felt toxic to her.

Lina took her purple shoes and her *What Is Love?* book and went out on the porch. Still mad at the handyman, I thought about Lina in the least favorable way. How come she hasn't been swimming in the pool yet? What do I have to do to convince her to have some fun?! Where is all this negativity coming from?

"Lina, I'm going to swim in the pool. You can do whatever you prefer. But I am not having another conversation about the car until we are going in it. Mark my word."

I heard my own thoughts and understood that thinking and focusing and acting from the point of view of what was wrong was simply creating more of the same. I heard the judgment in my words to her. I saw that Lina would do better without my adrenaline flowing all around her.

So I left her, crossed the lawn, and entered the gate to the pool, where Elsa and Natalia were diving and playing and laughing. And I relaxed. Slowly I began to feel the joy of the water and the sun washing through me. The anger about the handyman began to melt away, and I was beginning to feel playful and joyful again. Then I walked back to the house, sat down right in front of Lina where she was sitting with a short-term aide, Sarah, on the bench in the hallway, still waiting to go in the car. I smiled and looked Lina deep in her eyes.

"Lina, let's ask Sarah to make you one more fried egg while you and I go and check out the pool."

Lina looked at me. She smiled and took my hand. We walked quietly over to the pool. Elsa, Natalia, Lina, and I held one another's hands while standing on the edge, and on the count of three, we were all going to jump in. We all did, except Lina, who triumphantly stood by the edge as the rest of us all splashed into the pool.

"Lina! You tricked me!" I shouted. The game was on. Lina kept tricking us. Finally Elsa, always ahead of everything, decided to push both Lina and me into the pool. Everything was good again. We jumped, we sang, we splashed. Lina twirled around in the water.

"Lina, I love it when you are here. I really love playing and swimming and singing with you. I just love to have you around."

Lina reached out and touched my cheek. Her touch, when she is feeling good, has the vibration of a healer. I thought about Lina, about what it is in her that's so appealing. And I realized that a lot of it has to do with her ability to accept things and people the way they are. She is motivated by something much bigger and freer and more expansive than ego. When she is happy, she is so fully connected to herself and everyone around. She is pure presence.

* * *

"Only that which doesn't teach, which does not cry out, which does not condescend, which does not explain, is irresistible."

—WILLIAM BUTLER YEATS

Though, in her own way, with her own perfect timing, Lina does teach.

Donovan was hanging out with Lina in my apartment in the city. We had just eaten dinner, and Lina and Donovan were chilling out in her room listening to music before her calming and detoxifying Epsom salt bath. Lina, who wanted to swing high in her hammock and have some alone time, told Donovan "good-bye Donovan," "go home." She kept up her farewell comments until Donovan, speaking softly and sweetly as always, told her, "Lina, it hurts my feelings when you tell me to go home." Lina looked at Donovan, a tiny smile playing at the edges of her mouth as she responded:

"Be happy."

Her natural state—in spite of mycoplasma bacteria, PANDAS, inflammation, sensory discord, and everything else that came her way—is happiness and love.

When Lina feels secure with someone, and she knows they can handle her honesty, she gives them her straightforward, truthful messages. It's an invitation to love and play without ego interfering. It's an invitation to love oneself so much that those little straightforward technicalities that she dishes out now and then are a pee in the Nile compared to the overall love and appreciation that she expresses on a daily, hourly basis.

Lina wanted to listen to music. Marvin Gaye was one of Lina's top ten at this time, and Donovan, who shared Lina's appreciation, sang along as they listen together. Donovan is an amazing caretaker, an amazing friend to Lina, and a wonderful human being, but his singing just might not have caught up yet with the greatness of this young man.

"Quiet mouth," Lina said to Donovan after a couple of seconds of his sing-along, in the same matter-of-fact manner as she told me one night at dinner to "throw the soup in the garbage."

"Quiet mouth to who?" Donovan inquired.

"Quiet mouth to Donovan."

The beauty of Lina is that she doesn't hold onto things a second longer than she has to. And when her mental space allows her to take the opportunity of whatever she has in front of her, she goes for it. It's a very honest way of life. Donovan was walking with Lina back from Atlas all the way to Tony's house, fifty-two blocks away, on a Friday afternoon. Halfway through their walk, Lina got a little gloomy. It was a hot summer day in July, and she was beginning to lose steam. Lina showed the beginning signs of the growls and crying that we all are ever so familiar with. But instead of actually growling and crying, Lina started a little dialogue with herself, showing how she was beginning to internalize all the supports that she'd received when falling apart.

"Are you getting angry? Are you upset? No crying," she said.

It seemed like she was acknowledging the possibility of those feelings and how she wanted to express them, but that speaking them out loud was enough. She didn't have to act it all out. And then, instead of having to growl or cry, she was satisfied just to sit down on the bench next to Donovan and wait until the feelings passed.

* * *

Lina has so much magic in her, but not yet the appropriate motor pathways to express what she knows most of the time. I believe that once we spend less time in the city and more time in North Salem, where she's surrounded by nature and trees and grass and sky and moon and stars and wild birds, Lina will find enough allies in her environment to feel calm and centered enough to begin to express more of what she knows. It is already beginning to happen.

She says things suddenly, almost out of the blue. It happens when we are very connected, when she knows she has my full attention, when I am not distracted, not running around, not thinking about the next thing that I have to do.

"The girl in the pool saw the hawk."

"Mmm, she did, eh? What was the color of the hawk?"

"White."

It was long after the fact. A week or two. Lina processes time in a different way from most people. We had been swimming in the pool, and someone, I think it was Elsa, pointed out the white hawk circling over the pool and the field. Lina had not said anything. It didn't look like she had paid attention at all. But she had. And to her, it wasn't just a hawk. It was a power animal. I know when Lina talks about spirit animals. Don't ask me how, I can't answer that, but I know enough to know when she is talking about animals generally and spirit or power animals specifically.

I believe many, maybe all, of us have spirit animals by our side, and that their specific strengths, particularly when we become aware of their presence, help us to live our lives on a higher ground.

The hawk, according to the Native American tradition, is the messenger of the spirit world. Hawk medicine allows for the power to see, have a clear vision, focus, and take the lead when the time is right. Like most bird messengers, the hawk as a power animal is considered a messenger from the spirit world and from the world of that which we cannot see but have to intuit. Lina's awareness of the hawk, to me, is the beginning of a different kind of journey. As we spend time in the country with nature and wild animals all around us, we will see things we haven't seen before. Maybe Lina already sees these things, I don't know, but I do believe that this can be a place for her to find more words to describe what she sees, like the hawk, that most people only have a vague or nonexistent understanding of. And I believe that her insights can be helpful to many, just as they already have been to me.

CHAPTER EIGHT

Our North Salem Home Program

ATLAS, Lina's AMAZING school, is full of good-hearted, open-minded, warm, loving, intelligent, and fun teachers and staff, yes, but being in the city, it wasn't what I imagined as the most effective healing space for Lina. When we'd bought the North Salem house, I imagined that it would someday become more than a country house. It would become a full endeavor and Lina's new school.

Alison, cofounder and former codirector of Atlas, came for her first visit to North Salem one cold, snowy Tuesday afternoon right after the fence project was completed. We walked across the field together while I shared with her the vision that had been forming in my mind. I told her about my hope to allow Lina and possibly other students to move through their school day in close connection with nature, with animals, maybe some goats and chickens, possibly a horse. I talked to her about creating a learning environment where there would be no distinction between playing, working, and being a productive member of the community. How I envisioned Lina and her friends swinging, jumping in the high-ceilinged studio, planting and harvesting vegetables, berries, and herbs from the garden. We agreed that science was just as well taught in the kitchen as in a chair in front of a desk, and that math taught while jumping and swinging in the studio was more likely to fire off useful neurotransmitters than if we sat Lina down in front of papers with arbitrary numbers and circles and squares. We talked about social studies in the barn, artwork in the attic, music out in the field with drummers and guitars and goats and people, and NeuroMovement as part of the curriculum.

Alison agreed to help me start up with Lina in the fall of 2017. Alison, who lives in a land of enthusiasm and inspiration, was instantly on board with the idea that if we were to have students other than Lina, a common vision in the parents, rather than money, should be what determined who our students would be. I didn't want to create another program that only allowed access to kids with special needs whose parents had above-average resources. And I did not want to create yet another program that forced parents to put themselves in precarious financial situations in order to offer it to their children. Instead, I was hoping that it would be possible for the students to be there without leaving wrecked bank accounts in their wake and without having to answer to any department of education or other governmental agencies for Individualized Educational Programs (IEPs), funding, vaccine records, curriculum, etc. I was hopeful that if we built a good homeschool program that resulted in improved quality of life for the children and families we served, we would, no doubt, find good-hearted people who would wish to contribute and make this program accessible to whoever needed and wanted it the most.

Alison was all in. Everyone should have an Alison around when they want good energy, intelligence, and a spark igniting their vision. I thought about what Barbara Wosinski had said: "It will all just come to you. You don't have to try hard or make a big effort. Your tribe will show up. The land wants purpose, a new beginning. I see children running around, laughing." I saw that too, and I held onto her words about not having to make an effort. And here was Alison, who is amazing at all the things I am not great at. Administration. Permits. Spreadsheets. Deadlines. Regulations. Foundations. Forms. DOE. IHIP. 501(c)3 application. And she approaches all of it with a huge smile. She is an amazing teacher who looks at potential rather than limitation.

This focus, on strength rather than limitation, is exactly what I was looking for in potential collaborators. That Alison was as happy and enthusiastic as I was about the potential of our future North Salem Movement Center made it an easy decision for me to ask her to join me.

That summer, Alison started to come in for weekly Tuesday night dinners in North Salem as we planned starting North Salem Movement Center in September 2017. Lina would sit with us, smiling at the upbeat energy and the excited vibe that spread around the house like wildfire. I imagined the house and the farm and every room, every pasture being utilized to the maximum in a spirit of respect and curiosity. To me, the most important principle for this project was that there is great transformative power in simple appreciation. This idea, I hoped, would run like a river through every class, every meeting, every meal, every interaction. Lina does not need to be fixed. She does not need to be altered, improved, bettered. There is no right or wrong. There are some rules that have to do with safety and basic respect, sure, but we wouldn't relate to some behaviors as bad and some as good. We would honor and respect and appreciate where Lina and her potential friends are and understand that in their world they had good reason to be wherever they were at the moment. We wouldn't engage in correcting or lecturing or imposing on students or their parents or anyone else walking through the gate of this farm. There were already enough experts and specialists and lecturers out there. Most parents of special needs kids have a lot of experience in being talked down to, diminished, and demeaned. I wanted to have a place where special needs kids, their parents, and their siblings would feel free to tune into their own instincts, see the beauty in their own experience, and have the space to acknowledge how far they come and how well they've managed to get through often extremely challenging situations. Or, as Jamaican spiritual teacher Mooji expresses it:

In this instant,
There is nothing
To do or undo,
Nothing to change,
Nothing to fix,
Nothing to heal,
Nothing to become.

There is a natural
Sense of satisfaction
Or completeness,
Take full rest
In your Self.

We know so very little about what goes on inside a human. We cannot ever be certain about what our special kids know and don't know. They may see and feel and hear things we cannot yet access. We may find things through our special kids that we cannot find anywhere else. And that was the spirit in which I wanted to start up Lina's home program.

Through my journey with Lina, I have learned to become keenly interested in how my own thoughts, feelings, and energy impact everything that is going on in my life. Lina is acutely sensitive to people's energy. The way she responds to me when I feel free and happy, open and receptive is so different from when I feel stressed, frustrated, locked up, closed down. It's so much more fun to live life unconditionally. Lina, whose moods can shift on a dime, taught me that the best I can do for her when she spins into an anxious or agitated, obsessive place is to not join her in those feelings, but to keep caring about staying with my own center. We are so used to thinking that suffering on each other's behalf is the compassionate thing to do. I no longer believe that I am of any use to anyone if I join others in their feelings about their struggle. And I don't think worrying about anything or anyone is going to take me closer to a solution, mine or theirs.

One rainy morning in mid-May, before Alison and I had our meeting that led to the decision to homeschool Lina, I drove from New York City to Stamford, Connecticut, to attend a conference on the subject of the Law of Attraction. It was led by Abraham and Esther Hicks, who spread the teachings of how we are physical extensions of that which is nonphysical, how we are here because we choose to be here, how the purpose of our lives is joy and freedom. I walked into a conference room with seven hundred other participants. I sat down at one of the few available seats and looked around me. There was so much excitement and joy in this room. There's no way that I could describe who showed up to this kind of conference, the crowd was so diverse. I greeted the woman on my right. On my left was a black man with glasses, communicating to someone on his cell phone. I tried to catch his eye to say hi, but he was very focused on his phone. For whatever reason, and very uncharacteristic of me, I decided to try to get his attention.

"Hi."

No response.

"Hi and hello!"

Nothing. If anything, the man seemed to sink even deeper into his phone world.

"Hi, hello, and hello!" I said and touched his shoulder slightly.

The man gave up, turned to me with a big smile, and reciprocated my greetings.

I instantly felt his sweet, thoughtful energy and understood why I hadn't taken his no for an answer. He was there because his wife had bought him a ticket to the conference as they choose to live their lives with the notion that everything is possible and life is full of joy and happiness. He listened carefully to me when I described how I had gotten interested in the Abraham Hicks teachings through my experiences with Lina and how I wanted to develop my connection with her. His response showed me that he had no trouble following and applying awareness and compassion to whatever the subject.

"I get it, you are already doing it. But you want to keep working on your connection with Lina. It makes perfect sense to me."

He seemed excited when I told him I wanted to start some kind of home program for Lina and potentially other kids with special needs. I felt genuinely excited for him and his wife when I heard about their plans to have a baby. Somehow, I felt like I knew him already.

"So where do you come from?" I asked, knowing that many participants had traveled far to this gathering, which seems to sell out in every part of the country.

"I'm from Brewster, how about you?"

"Really! My ex-husband and I just bought a house in North Salem!"

"That's where we live!"

"You are kidding!?

"June Road."

It was a Law of Attraction moment. June Road is a cross street to Bloomer Road. And what Antwaine then told me was no longer surprising, because deep inside, I have known for a long time that North Salem will come with a tribe. And this tribe is nothing that I have to fight for, it will just happen.

"I don't know much about autism and education, but I do have two hands, and I want to help you with your school."

I looked at this gentle, thoughtful man and imagined his wife by his side, someone who had the wherewithal and the generosity to send her husband to an uplifting conference even though she couldn't attend herself. I thought, *this is going to be good; my tribe is on its way.*

Not all my tribe members are as close as Antwaine and Tiffany. Rupert Isaacson, of the Horse Boy method, was an important inspiration to me in starting Lina's home program. Rupert's oldest son had challenges similar to Lina's. Horses had always been a big part of Rupert's life, but in the context of discovering that his son's language, eye contact, and general well-being all improved when riding, he began to develop a program for kids on the spectrum based on movement. Horses and riding, jumping, swimming, and swinging all stimulated learning, Rupert discovered, much more effectively than sitting in a chair in front of a desk, trying to resolve abstract problems. The Horse Boy method, similar to the Son-Rise method and Greenspan's floor time approach, is based on finding the child's own motivation to learn and connect. Whatever the child is interested in is the focus of the teachings.

The first time I spoke with Rupert on the phone, I noticed how driven he was about everything related to the Horse Boy method. He is a great presenter, and, while he's exceedingly open and generous with time he doesn't have and is empathic and loving, he is a leader, no question. A little bit like an unstoppable train. Not a train wreck, but unstoppable. With his long, wild blond hair and lively, light blue eyes, his self-assured swagger, his cowboy boots, and big smile, he was exactly the way I had imagined when I met him for the first time at Newark Airport. He had come to New York to start up a Horse Boy/Movement method in connection with a college in Queens. The next three days became one long marathon discussion of healing, autism, Horse Boy method, life, shamanism. Soon, everyone at Atlas was participating in a short Horse Boy method training as well, and in June of 2017, Elsa and I made a trip to Austin, Texas, to study the method firsthand. I wanted to incorporate the Horse Boy method into Lina's home program in North Salem. Elsa had raised $500 for the Horse Boy Foundation. As Rupert and I became friends, Elsa had developed her own relationship with him and had decided, completely on her own initiative, that it was something she wanted to support. She had lemonade stands on 81st Street and West End Avenue on New York City's Upper West Side. She had lotteries with homemade art pieces. And when she wrote Rupert a letter to describe why she wanted to support his program, he wrote her back and asked her to come see what they did and choose how she wanted the $500 to be utilized.

So, Elsa and I took our first trip together to Rupert's horse farm in Texas. She had her first horseback ride on the trails around the farm. We felt the warm, compassionate, and enthusiastic energy of everyone working and playing on the farm, and we flew back home, inspired. I knew that I would need someone on the farm to help take care of day-to-day operations, mowing the field, snowplowing in winter, building an outdoor obstacle course, and, of course, mending the fence that needed ongoing repair, fixing things that break, building the chicken coop, and all the little things that I was trying to tend to while also working on chasing away Lina's mycoplasma bacteria, caring for my two daughters, developing my new NeuroMovement career to work with kids with special needs, seeing my psychotherapy clients, writing, and still having time to myself to play. There just weren't enough hours in the day, and I realized I needed help. Roshelle's impending departure sparked an idea. I needed more than one person; I needed two. I needed a couple. One of them would work on the farm, and the other would help me care for Lina. I thought it would be amazing to have a couple who were happy to be in beautiful nature, loved to work, loved each other, understood what we were doing there, and felt something about being a part of it.

I wanted to find that special couple by August, a month before our home program began in the fall with Lina. As the end of July rolled around, I had the idea to ask some people that I had come across in the process of renovating our house. One such person, Fabio, had helped me put up a few heavy things on the wall and hang swings all around the house. He texted me back and said he thought he might have someone for me. At the same time, the person who had helped with the process of removing lead paint and repainting the whole house, inside and outside, said that one of his best friends was interested in the job, as well.

The following weekend, my friend Agnes and I were up at the house for the weekend with our kids. Both candidates came by to learn more about our project and whether they would be right for the job. We were all out in the yard having a picnic and our kids were running around barefoot on the grass when Tales and his wife, Carla, walked up the driveway with big smiles on their faces. I looked at the two of them, their friendly faces and their natural, warm demeanor, and knew this was what I had been looking for. I explained our vision and walked with them around the land, watching their excitement grow as we explored the stable, the guesthouse, the huge field in front of the house, and the studio that I was in the process of turning into a giant, educational playhouse. Tales hypothesized about being part of building something that could be beneficial to Lina and others, and Carla, his beautiful, soft-spoken wife, just smiled, knowingly. By the time my other candidate, a tall, dark, striking man in his thirties and Brazilian like Tales and Carla, knocked on my door later that evening, I had already made my decision. We had found gold. I walked with him from house to house and told him about my plans, and he was polite but didn't seem genuinely excited about the possibilities. I thanked him for his time and walked back into the house knowing that everything was going to be okay.

A few weeks later, Tales and Carla moved into the guesthouse at our North Salem house. A month after that, right after Labor Day, Lina started her first school day at the farm.

Tony and I had taken the girls to Miami Beach the week before. The mycoplasma bacteria were back in full swing. OCD and a relentlessly triggered amygdala turned all four days into a challenge that almost felt unearthly. Riddled with agitation, Lina kept asking for whatever she didn't have. She wanted the Uber car when we were taking a taxi. She wanted the hotel room when we were in the pool. After having asked for the blue ocean every day all through the winter and spring, I never thought I would witness the day when Lina wouldn't go in it. But here it was, the day when Lina refused to go into the ocean. She was miserable. I saw Elsa cringe at the mere stress of listening to one massive OCD episode after another, from morning to evening and way into the night. At one point, overwhelmed by her own acute anxiety state, Lina hit me with both of her hands right in my face, full force. I felt my neck jerk in an unnatural direction. But more than that, I felt a sinking feeling, a difficulty holding onto the idea that there was a point to all of this. I wanted to have the right to give up. I said to myself, I do have the right to give up. And that somehow helped me. We came back to the city, Lina OCDing the entire way home about wanting to go into the ocean, and life just kept going on.

On September 5th, 2017, we had our first day at our North Salem Movement and Learning Center, with Tales, Carla,

Alison, and Elsa, whose school didn't start until the following week. That evening, we had a first day of school dinner celebration. Elsa put together little flower packages for everyone and made lemonade with stevia; Lina ran from the table to the refrigerator, trying to snatch some extra olives when no one was watching. That day came and went, and the next one and the next, until one day, during Lina's second week of home program, her OCD subsided dramatically, and a calm came over her that I hadn't seen for years. Could it really be about the calm and peace out here? I felt a deep satisfaction, a conviction that this was the right thing to do. And then, one night as Lina and I sat in her bedroom talking and flipping through magazines, she turned to me and said, unsolicited:

"I love you, Mom."

Lina's bedtime began to change from 11 or 12 to 10:30 or even 10. Her immediate reaction to being out here for these early days of her new home program reinforced my trust in the healing effect of nature and calm. We spend so much time in overstimulating places that we somehow think that we need to be almost overpowered by stimulation to get tired. We somehow get it in our confused minds that we need to exhaust our kids with endless input or else they won't be able to learn or rest. We drown them in words and information and sensory input and hope that they will retain some of it and make use of it and don't realize that the very volume of what we offer makes it almost impossible for them to retain any of it. We think we have to struggle to get rewards. We think we have to expend effort to see results. I have lived most of my life powering through obstacles. As I get older, I see that there is another way, a quiet way, a softer, easier way.

For a while after our Miami trip, I still had those thoughts of wanting to give up. Maybe I needed to detach myself now and then to be able to step back, stop trying, fighting, struggling. But one night, as Elsa, who is almost always happy, cried when she told me about difficulties she was having with her new friends at her new middle school, I realized that walking around disillusioned, like a quitter, wasn't going to work, either. Much of that night after I put Elsa to bed, I was up worrying about everything between the sun and the moon, until I woke up in the morning with a decision. It didn't matter if I had the right to my feelings or not. It didn't matter if I was justified, if it was understandable, or even expected. Giving up just wasn't going to work for Elsa and Lina. It wasn't going to be fun or good for them. So, I decided like so many times before to go back to being happy and enjoying everything as much as I possibly could. And Elsa sat down with me early in the morning on the couch as soon as I was done with my meditation and told me that she was done being upset about kids excluding her. She would find other friends. She already had some good friends at the school and many outside of school, and it was all going to work out.

Elsa never holds onto anything. She processes things quickly and honestly, and then she just finds her joy again and moves on to the next thing. She really wants to be happy. She cares about what she feels and what comes out of her mouth. She never lingers in negative places. She is like the sun; she just wants to shine. She has that happy-go-lucky energy, that sunny, in-the-moment, celebratory festive shine that makes you want to have her around all the time. That afternoon, Elsa came back from school with three new friends. That's how she operates. If something doesn't work for her, instead of lingering over it, she goes off and finds something better.

Elsa's positive energy reminds me about what I love about dogs. Dogs just want to be happy, and they usually are. For a while, I'd been looking for a dog, because I believe that the presence of a dog will be a constant reminder of how to live in the moment and be happy and carefree, but the right dog hasn't come our way yet. All the dogs we've considered adopting were either too timid, or traumatized, or anxious. One dog got sick right before she was to be shipped to us. I wondered why it wasn't working out and came to the conclusion that the time hadn't been right. Tony thought I was crazy to think about getting a dog during these challenging times.

"Why don't we adopt a couple of extra kids too, while we are at it?"

I half knew he was right and half thought he was wrong. More is not necessarily more difficult. I knew we would eventually find the right dog. I imagined that it would just be something that came to us, maybe even literally, walking into our North Salem farm one day. Kind of like getting pregnant without planning it, you get to bypass all the ambivalence and fear about the life-changing responsibilities of having a child.

During the summer before Lina's home program started, we had borrowed a friend's house in Edgartown on Martha's Vineyard. The owners of the house had a beautiful Husky, who, apart from the fact that she was a talented Houdini-resembling escape artist, was Buddha-like, and extremely patient and loving. Lina, who much prefers larger dogs to little yapping ones with Napoleon complexes, had gotten used to this gentle, large Husky girl in a matter of hours. She slept for thirteen hours straight for two days in a row, not necessarily unrelated to the calming energy of this dog. Brook, which was Houdini-dog's real name, did escape twice, but her loving ways seemed to instantly erase any memory of her misdemeanors. When we left to drive back to New York, I cried.

A spunky, good-hearted dog trainer, former New York City resident Mickey who now spends her days with multiple dogs on a farm upstate, is continuously on the lookout for the right dog for our family. She emailed me one day about a dog, Max, that had recently been transported from Florida to a horse farm near us, for a period of fostering before hopefully being adopted. I made five phone calls about this dog and sent a few Facebook messages without any results. When I finally got a hold of the farm, I learned that Max had already been adopted. But I was told that they had two other dogs that were rescued post-hurricane Irma from South Carolina. One was Gloria.

We jumped in the car to meet her. As soon as we drove up the farm's driveway, Gloria, a golden short-haired mixture of things with a black nose and gorgeous, brown eyes, came shooting out of the barn. She jumped straight into our car.

Barbara, the farm manager, suggested Gloria come to our home for a visit. Lina had had a particularly difficult day, because, in addition to all her other challenges, she also has a profound sensitivity to ragweed, and it was everywhere on our farm. Lina wasn't exactly in the best frame of mind to make Gloria's first visit to our farm a harmonious one. But Gloria didn't seem the slightest bit worried. She ran around the premises with Elsa like she owned the place, wandering around the rooms in the house as if she were trying to find her personal resting space. When Lina calmed down, Gloria took the liberty of jumping up on the couch next to her and kissing her from her face all the way down to her toes.

I saw how good this dog was. But I also knew how much work was required to keep Lina's home program running. Gloria had skin allergies. That didn't worry me. She also limped and had sensitive paws. That did concern me. Barbara, who must be an angel, understood the dilemma of taking on a dog with health problems in the context of Lina's challenges and suggested that we have Gloria over whenever we wanted to without making any commitment until they found out more about Gloria's physical health.

"I think your ultimate goal is to have a dog," she said. "So, whether it's Gloria or some other dog, it may be good for you to have her around now and then, whenever you want to, as a first step. You are welcome to come visit her and play with her at the farm anytime, and I can drive Gloria here and pick her up when you need me to."

I looked at this gentle woman with soft kindness beaming out of her eyes, who herself had two dogs and three children, and thought about how amazing the universe is. How whenever I am about to get a dog, some obstacle gets in the way, as if the universe is saying to me, "Helena, I know you want a dog, but look at your life. Look at how you are still running around trying to heal your daughter, running a home program now, doing NeuroMovement with other people's special needs children on weekends, building fences and clearing hiking paths, trying to build a meaningful, joyful existence for Lina, and at the same time needing to have enough energy to provide for Elsa." I decided to take this opportunity to get to know a dog without having to take on more responsibilities. I thanked Barbara for everything she does for one rescue dog after another, as well as for our family by appreciating our situation and offering a gradual solution.

As promising as the first two weeks of our home program in North Salem were (the best since the upsurge of Lina's mycoplasma infection a year and a half earlier), the third week was as disastrous. Tales and I set upon the ragweed, determined to eradicate it. We pulled the plants from the soil with a vengeance, thinking that it would make a difference to Lina's state of mind. I can't say that I know how ragweed works. How far the pollen travels, how the weed spreads. Truth is, I don't know much about farming or gardening. And when it comes to autism, it is the biggest mystery and source of confusion that I have come across in my lifetime. What I do know, however, is that pulling those particular weeds out of the ground, before I had to face that it might not make much of a difference to Lina, made me very happy. It is not every day that an autism mother, or father, comes across a potentially concrete solution to any aspect of their child's suffering. I could have pulled them out of the ground for a week. I didn't feel tired, and I didn't notice until the day after that my arms were completely scratched up and I had a poison ivy rash on both of my wrists. But it was all worth it for the empowering idea that Lina would do better without the offending plant.

Parents of kids with autism are always trying to find answers, always asking how to best relate to their children. My underlying approach is always consistency, conveying that yelling doesn't make the world stop and bring you what you want, that moving your body in dramatic ways, flailing your arms, and throwing a couple of cups of water across the room won't bring anyone closer to their ice cream or whatever ice cream is to them in their world. I try not to give in to Lina's demands when she screams and shouts. I try to stay empathetic and consistent at the same time.

Still, there isn't exactly a recipe for how to relate to one's special kid's challenges, or a manual that tells you what behavior stems from mycoplasma infection and what behavior has been learned over the years of parents' sadness and guilt about not being able to help their child more. That whenever our children fall apart, we have strong reactions whether we say something or stay silent, whether we try to stop it, hide it, stay impartial to it, or simply just survive it. I sometimes wake up in the middle of the night and think that I hear her scream, until I realize it was just a kind of cellular memory and Lina is actually sleeping soundly and quietly in her room. Even in my awake state, I hear screams that happened hours, even days ago.

The question I keep asking myself through these storms is "Can I or can I not be happy in spite of what my child is going through?" These kinds of impossible situations, of screaming, popping her hips in that way that feels catastrophic, repeating, *Can I please have an uber car, can I please go to papa's house, can I please go to mama's house, can I please have the blue car, can I please have white breakfast* and *no! no!* and more *no*, feel like a kind of death. It triggers thoughts about the surreal nature of the sheer negativity and intensity of the situation that turns into a feeling of this being a bad life. Why am I spelling this out? Because I think every parent with a child on the spectrum, whatever that means, recognizes something in these thought patterns.

For me, most of the time, the more difficult it is to be happy in spite of the challenges, the more determined I get. Guilt is very often in the way of my happiness. It's an emotion that is extremely hard to deal with for me and, I suspect, for any parent who has a child with serious challenges. And yet, guilt leads to more suffering, in the parent as well as in the child. It definitely leads to less desirable interactions. Guilt is five extra thick logs straight into the autism fire. We give our children excuses to operate on unacceptable levels instead of expecting more and seeing them as equals. We overcompensate by oversupporting them, over-protecting them, overloving them, overdoing everything and leaving them with less. Maybe we would be machines if we didn't have these tendencies. But this overcompensation is not effective, and it's so freeing every time we let that guilt go, because it's in the way of being connected with our kids in a happy, free, authentic way. Guilt makes us put up with things that we wouldn't put up with had we trusted ourselves and our children more. It gets us into masochistic patterns with our children, and that makes us less interested in spending time with them.

Many years ago, when I was a college student, I had a bike accident. A car ran into me and my bike, and I flew off the bike and landed on the ground. I woke up from being unconscious many hours later. From the accident, I had the kind of head-aches that forced me to take a break from my studies. I decided to move to New York City, where I thought that the mere intensity of this large, colorful city would help me stop focusing on the pain. I also decided that the pain wasn't the boss of me. I wasn't going to use it as an excuse to be miserable, irresponsible, or passive. It was the gift that I decided to give to myself that would make it all better. When I think about Lina's struggles, so much more profound than mine were, I want to give her this gift, too. Or at the very least, not be the one who takes away her opportunities to give herself this gift. Ultimately, I think this is one of the most respectful ways that we can be with each other. Trusting each other's competence, resilience, power, and ability to make good choices for ourselves. Not trying to save each other. Not overcompensating for what we feel is a limitation in another person. Seeing strength, not weakness. Seeing possibility, not limitation.

Part of the advantage of having a home program is that I have full freedom to do what I believe best promotes Lina's well-being and happiness. Her ability for a fuller expression is something I believe is one of the fundamentals.

I always knew Lina had everything inside of her. An intact intellect, a full thought process, and deep understanding: cognitive, emotional, and social. I never for a second believed the psychologist hired by the DOE to evaluate Lina who evaluated my then-eleven-year-old daughter's intelligence as equal to that of a three-year-old and, described her as "mentally retarded" (yes, that was his exact articulation).

Lina dropped little hints whenever I stared too hard at her compromised language and began to adapt mine to what was tangible and concrete. It's no excuse, but everyone around Lina, and almost everyone who relates to nonverbal children, does this. We are so dependent on evidence, and our intuition is constantly dismissed, ignored, and doubted. But with our nonverbal children, our kids on the spectrum in particular, we have to rely on our inner knowing. We need to get great at listening to our own most sane inner voice and trust it. We have to look into our kids' eyes and recognize that they are all there, no matter what comes out of their mouths. I knew that Lina was an aware, fully comprehending human being. And that's where RPM, Rapid Prompting Method, comes in.

It was created by Soma Mukhopadhyay, when she raised and taught her son, Tito, who was diagnosed with severe autism at the age of three. With the help of RPM, Tito is now a young adult and a writer and poet, the author of *The Mind Tree: A Miraculous Child Breaks the Silence of Autism*. Soma worked tirelessly on reading, prompting Tito to point to numbers and letters, and by six years old, Tito was writing independently. By twelve years of age, Tito wrote his first book, *Beyond the Silence*.

Soma now teaches students all around the United States. Neuroscientist Michael Merzenich, PhD, professor at the University of California, San Francisco, a researcher at the W.M. Keck Center for Integrative Neuroscience, and author of *Soft Wired* (2013), studied Tito specifically to learn more about autism and the brain.

RPM uses letter boards and other very simple tools to elicit spelling and expression in students. It's a teaching method first, which eventually leads to fluent expressive language in the student. The provider presents a lesson on a topic that's likely to interest the student and eventually allows the student to insert themselves into the topic, directly and indirectly, by listening, answering questions, pointing to choices, and eventually spelling whole words and sentences. The method assumes competence, not necessarily knowledge, in the student. It is extremely respectful of the student's sensory needs, privacy, and history. Going very gradually from a general topic to more personal expressions allows the student to feel less overwhelmed and pressured than in immediately open-ended communications as presented in many other forms of facilitated communication.

The first time I sat in with Lina during her lesson with Jane Potthaust, a pretty young woman providing RPM for children in the New York and Connecticut area, Lina ended her lesson spelling out "love mom." Over Elsa's spring break, I brought her with us for one of Jane's lessons. When asked to give a word that she associated with her sister, Lina spelled "happy." It's like Christmas every time we go to see Jane.

When Lina started spelling things out on the stencil with holes in the shape of letters, pointing with a pen through the letter that would take her to the words and the sentences trapped in her own mind, it was a jaw-dropping experience. It is so miraculous to hear your child as an independent, sophisticated thinker after years, over a decade, of "can I please have the blue car with my yellow mom!" "go to Trader Joe's," "purple oliiiiives!!" It's surreal to hear her suddenly point to letters that spell out words like "Matisse," "funny," "weird," etc. Spelling the word *desolate* as a synonym for empty, commenting that a particular Greek myth strikes her as "very intriguing" and that "conquer" is the same as "taking over" finally show us the inside of Lina's beautiful mind. She can follow and reflect on the story of Joan of Arc and describe the "mystical" and "spiritual" aspects of this unusual and powerful historical figure. She can follow along complex ideas of art history and show her understanding of cubism, impressionism, and realism. She can write about volcanos. And when her hands and eyes aren't cooperating well with her mind, she can spell out "I am not trying to space out." I keep wondering what it must be like to be so thoroughly misunderstood by everyone around her while knowing that her own mind reflects none of what is coming out of her own mouth.

Jane became an RPM provider because her brother has autism and found a way to express himself through the method. Her soft voice and gentle demeanor are no reflection of a lack of determination. She calmly reads educational stories and requests that Lina spell out her understanding of the world, history, science, and art, even when Lina gets up and tries to push her away or charges for the door. Sometimes, Jane even pushes Lina back into the chair when she tries to escape. Lina's shouting about wanting to go to the blue car or "go make a pee-pee" is met with, "yes, pee" and followed by the immediate return to whatever subject was interrupted by Lina's anxious OCD. Ultimately, it's understood by the RPM professionals that being understood, spelling, and expressing one's understanding and thoughts about a wide range of subject matters is in itself therapeutic.

After having expressed her very real understanding of the difference between realist and abstract painters, Lina leaves Jane's tiny office on the second floor of a Methodist church in Fairfield, Connecticut (or Jane's own office in a high-rise building on Cadman Plaza in Brooklyn), with the calm and confidence of someone who just passed the bar exam, got promoted or proposed to, or was awarded for some great or brave endeavor. And I walk out of whichever office we can catch Jane in, with an equal feeling of just having won the lottery, in awe of my teenage girl's ability to keep on living in a world that has absolutely no clue who she is.

When Jane told us that Soma Mukhopadhyay was going to be teaching in Long Island in the fall, I knew we had to meet her. As we walked into the building on a hot day in September, the parents who had organized Soma's visit greeted us warmly by our names. Soma, a very petite but sturdy-looking Indian woman in a sari, greeted us and led us into a small, brightly lit room with a couple of chairs, a desk, and a video camera. Lina's initial curiosity soon turned into anxiety. She began raising her voice and said "no" to every one of Soma's suggestions to hold the pencil and point to the letter on the stencil to spell the word in question, something she had done for Jane many times. Soma talked about trees; Lina shouted about wanting to "go with yellow, pink mom to the blue car." Soma patiently continued her lesson, prompting Lina to answer questions. Lina eventually responded, pointing her pencil at the letter board Soma held up, spelling the words *anxious, clock, after,* and *tree* like a champ and solving math problems in a matter of seconds that I would stay bewildered by for hours, all the while popping her hips and yelling louder.

"Interesting," Soma commented somberly and carried on her lesson.

"I want the blue car with mom!" Lina shouted.

"You will not get to the blue car until you do this work."

"No! No! I won't! No blue car! No Soma! No you won't go in the blue car! No point to the letter!"

"You do all that drama," Soma said in her thick Indian accent, "I know you are anxious but I am telling you, if you don't do this work, you will have to stay here and clean all these rooms and not go in the blue car until it's done."

I couldn't hold back a spontaneous laugh. This little lady wasn't the slightest bit impressed by Lina's behaviors, and I felt a sense of calm settle over me. I realized that even if I try to be consistent with Lina, and never give in to what she is yelling for, I avoid asking her for things that I fear will make her anxious and upset. And I overcompensate and anticipate what she cannot do. However much I try to be cool and respectful of Lina, I overlove her, and I feel sorry for her when she falls apart rather than expecting her to stop. I saw everything between Lina and me as I was sitting there watching this little powerhouse of a lady. I saw myself, Lina, how we got there, how we could move on from there, and the potential freedom and possibility that were there for us.

We drove home in silence. That evening, Lina was particularly affectionate with Elsa, actively reaching out to her. And to me, too. I think my pulling back gave her more space. I wasn't chasing her down because of my guilt and sadness over her challenges. I saw her as my feisty, fully thinking and feeling individual in need of space and respect. The next day, I showed Elsa the video from our visit with Soma. Elsa cried, as she often does when she sees Lina falling apart. I talked about my recent discoveries, that ever since the Miami trip, I had found myself moving in the direction of letting Lina be Lina, letting things go, letting things fall apart, trying to learn not to fix things but trusting even more that Lina has the solution inside herself and I don't have to chase her down to find it.

Elsa, as profound as this child is and always has been, talked about not knowing how to be with Lina without trying. How she is scared that if she didn't try 200 percent to keep her closeness with Lina alive, there would be nothing there and she would lose Lina even more.

"I want to stop trying, I really, really do. But I don't know if I can."

"Elsa, my love, whatever you feel that you can do or can't do is perfect. Whatever you are feeling is perfect. We all have our own way to figure ourselves out in our own time."

Back in North Salem, Lina had another challenging day. She yelled and screamed and ran away from Carla into my room where I was working. I knew if I let Lina come shouting and screaming into my room whenever she was out of sorts, my life in North Salem wasn't going to work. So I stood up from my chair, simply picked her up from my bed where she was curled up under my blanket still yelling, dropped her outside my door, and closed my door with a firm bang. Lina instantly calmed down, went to her own room and her own bed, curled up, and relaxed. When I was done with my work and found her and Carla still in Lina's room, Lina still enjoying her own bed, I hugged her and tickled her and Lina chuckled like she had never experienced sorrow in her whole life.

Then we had a peaceful morning and one of our most amazing NeuroMovement lessons ever, with Lina lying quietly on the table, listening to her own system. Afterward, on our daily hike at a nearby nature preserve that we all now just refer to as "Baxter Road," I said to Lina:

"I love Baxter Road."

"I love Baxter Road too."

What is the big deal? She just added three letters? No, she entered into an expressive dialogue where she wasn't just requesting something, wasn't imitating anyone (though I don't mind and I do think this is a crucial part of the learning a language), wasn't contradicting anything, wasn't reaching for anything, but simply joining me in appreciation of Baxter Road.

We did almost daily NeuroMovement lessons, and I wondered, in addition to being up here with nature all around and apart from pulling out all the ragweed, if NeuroMovement was part of what helped Lina calm down. I have mostly worked with Lina when she is lying in her own bed, about to wake up, or about to fall asleep. Or when I find her sitting somewhere and I can sit down casually in front of her or behind her and start touching gently along her spine. Since we had begun our home program, Lina's NeuroMovement lessons became official and regular, on the table, in the NeuroMovement room. And when I have asked her, "does this feel ok?" or "still comfortable?" or "how does this feel?" she has consistently responded with "good," or "feels good," or even "yes, it feels good." And after the lessons she consistently seemed calmer and more centered, which simply wasn't the case after previous lessons. One day, because Elsa had a day off school and we had gone to a pumpkin festival instead of doing our usual NeuroMovement lesson and Baxter Road hike, Lina asked to be "on the bench, on my belly, with mom!"

Over this past year, my NeuroMovement practice, exclusively with children with special needs, simply flowed to me. Anat

Baniel's most trusted colleague, Marcy Lindheimer, works with special children from all over the world, whenever she is not involved in training practitioners. It turns out Marcy lives on my street on the Upper West Side. She became my mentor. When I started the training, I had no aspirations to work with other people's children. It was just something I did for Lina.

Whereas Lina had sometimes lost patience with the lessons in the past, she likes the NeuroMovement room and began to come along willingly every time I told her it was time to have a lesson. And whenever the lesson was over, Lina didn't want it to end. "No more 'lesson is over'" she would say and stay on the bench, until she realized that the next fun thing we would do was to drive up to the hiking area by Baxter Road and wander around the lake and across the fields and hills, talking about colors, people, and good food.

It's an ideal situation with Marcy. I watch her work with a child, then she sends the child to me for a couple of lessons or for a number of lessons over a few weeks. The child goes back for another master lesson with Marcy that I observe, then I have the chance to work for another week or two with the child, and so on. I work less and less as a psychotherapist and more and more as a NeuroMovement practitioner. Marcy never makes a big deal of herself. She is motivated by love for the children she works with and their parents, rather than ego. It's a unique opportunity to be able to watch a true master work with the same child as I do. When I observe Marcy's work, I have a hard time knowing what comes from her and what comes from her young student on her table. Her touch is so subtle, so tuned in and perceptive, it seems like it becomes part of the child's own movement. And every time I walk out of Marcy's office after watching another lesson of pure magic, I feel so grateful to her, to Lina, and to life for how well everything works out if we just let it.

Another thing that changed as soon as I started up Lina's home program in North Salem was that I felt closer to her. Maybe it had to do with my own feeling of finally doing what I knew was the right thing. My guilt about sending Lina downtown to a congested area of New York City for her schooling, when I knew she needed to be in a natural, more peaceful and harmonious environment, was gone. I knew, and I still know, this is the right thing for Lina. And while there have been challenging days on and off up here as well, there have been far more peaceful, deeply connected, joyful, much more expressive days already, and it is clear that Lina is responding positively to this major change in her life. It's not just Lina, but me, too. I get to spend day after day in the country, hiking with my daughter, building a chicken fence or a bed frame for Lina, or pulling ragweed, or fixing up the gym with Tales, whenever I am not working and Lina is busy learning with Alison or Carla.

"Lina," I told her one day when we were wandering around the lake up at Baxter Road, our daily hiking spot. "I really love these walks with you." Lina smiled.

"You know, I don't know who this whole North Salem project is helping the most, you or me."

And I mean that. Somehow, our deepest dreams are fulfilled through the process of helping our children. During the weeks that followed our start of the home program in North Salem, Lina now and then would turn to me and say, "Thank you." Sometimes she would even send a message through Donovan, who now worked with Lina more regularly, whenever she was at Tony's house in the city. She would ask him to text me and say, "Thank you mom." One night, Lina was lying in her bed, peaceful after a couple of back and foot rubs. She held her hand around my cheek, smiled with a kind of humorous, soft sweetness that you simply don't find in people very often, and said, "Leave the door open." She wanted me to leave, but the way that she told me made me feel anything but rejected. Moments like that, Lina acts like a master of relationships, a healer, someone who is completely confident and knowledgeable and intuitive in how to interact with others. It's as if autism is the furthest thing from the truth in those moments. It's as if I suddenly can see into her and get a sense of who she really is.

There is never a time when Lina seems more at peace, closer to herself, lighter, and happier than during our hikes at Baxter Road, a five-minute car ride from our farm. Every day is a new level of magic. It reminds me of what Malidoma, the divination shaman whom we met with a few years before, said about Lina. He said we needed to take her to magnificent places of natural beauty so that she can have reassurance from the outside of what she experiences on the inside but can't quite express in words. We leave the car on the side of the gravel road that brought us to the nature preserve, and within the first few steps on the trail, Lina starts breathing differently. Smiling. Standing still, looking around, as if she were taking in all the greatness. Her face relaxes. Her posture changes, her shoulders drop, and at the same time her spine seems to lengthen out as if she were reaching up toward the sky, alongside the old trees that are standing tall and magnificent all around her. She takes off, swinging her arms like pendulums, her big hair flowing in the wind; she turns around, laughing, waiting for me to catch up, leans in, kisses my cheek; she looks around, listens, takes a deep breath, and then is off to another leap forward, her long arms swinging high and low. There is no other place on Earth that I would rather be than with her out on those hilly, open fields and little paths inside wooded areas, both of us returning to a kind of human normalcy where life's ceiling feels much higher, much less limited. It's easier to breathe, easier to let go, easier to be at the only place worth being, which is right there, where words and theories and analyses and opinions no longer matter, where, if everything stopped at that moment, the contrast between this physical life and Great Spirit is much less extreme.

Sometimes, when Lina can't go to sleep, uncomfortable in some way or restless or anxious, I talk to her about this. I say all the things that she knows so much more about than I do but that I say anyway, because I believe it's reassuring for her to hear another person acknowledging the other dimensions.

"I love you, Lina," I start, "and whatever it is you are feeling at this moment, it's all going to pass. We are just here to play. We are just here to experience all these physical sensations and figure out how to live in balance with our physical and nonphysical parts and figure out what makes us happy."

If I said this to someone else, they might ask me, "What do you mean?" For Lina, this is just a reminder.

"Lina, I know you know all this. I know you know that the thing that is most true about you is that you are free. That this is temporary. You are just here because you want to play and experience what it is like to be in this kind of crazy world. This is nothing that will break you. You know this. We have everything. We are full of light. We are light. We can do anything we want. We are free and we will always be free and whatever happens here doesn't matter much. We can just play with it; we can just take it in and let it flow in and out of us like the wind . . ."

And like a very old lady whose physical existence got so limited that she had to open up to her internal spaciousness, Lina lies there, quietly listening to the words she understands so well, her face softening, her breath deepening, her torso sinking into the mattress, ready to let go and rest.

Sometime that winter, I ran into another mother in the city whom I had met a few years back. I watched her as she was standing there on the sidewalk. Something in her eyes was not lit up. Her posture appeared really heavy. The words came out of her mouth as if she had to use every ounce of effort to say hello and stay engaged with me. I knew that heavy feeling, the sense that life was asking too much of her, that there was no respite, nothing coming in, no end to the madness. I looked at her tired posture and wanted to offer real help as she told me about her son's violent outbursts. But I knew that she was part of a very complicated system that didn't easily lend itself to temporary outside assistance. And temporary, in all honesty, was all I would be able to offer.

It comes and goes, that feeling that one's legs are too heavy to shuffle forward. I think we have to acknowledge ourselves wherever we are. Feel our feelings. Open our hearts to everything that comes our way, even our despair, even our fear, our loss of hope. Whatever it is. Feel it fully and move on. Watch it, feel the energy of it, allow it to run its course through our systems, without making long, drawn-out stories about it, cry if we need to, be quiet, be loud, be mad, be sad all while watching it, knowing that, ultimately, none of it is who we are. It's just thought, energy, something that comes and goes. It's too much pressure to try to fight one's own reaction to whatever life is. To try to reason oneself out of something just never works. Self-care, for me, is to say to myself that whatever I am feeling and whatever thoughts I have about something is nothing more or less than that, thoughts and feelings. As I am watching all of my experiences and all of my thoughts and reactions to them, I ultimately know none of that is me. I am, like Michael Singer writes about in his 2013 book, *The Untethered Soul,* the one who watches it all come and go without identifying with any of it.

I have to remind myself to stop trying so hard. My friends make jokes about how tired it makes them to watch me run around. They say, "I don't know how you do it." It would be better for me, and for them too, I guess, if they could say, "I do see how you are doing it. I see how it all works out for you. I see that you have found some kind of balance."

I want to live that kind of life. A balanced life. A life full of self-acceptance. With rest and work and solid boundaries, with fun and calm and good food, and good friends, and time to see them. With love and closeness. With lots of joking around, with ping-pong, boxing, and building with one's own hands something cool, like an outdoor obstacle course for my kids. With nonketogenic meals a little more often. Without getting caught up in my own stories, with being able to hold onto the bigger picture, understanding my place on this planet, as something both much bigger and much smaller than my overactive mind tells me it is.

In a conversation with Barbara Wosinski, the alternative healer mentioned earlier, she told me that my kids are doing well. Both Lina and Elsa are happy. "Why are you putting so much pressure on yourself?" "Yes, why?" an internalized voice asked. Because in the world of autism mothering, there is a whole different meaning of "a woman's work is never done." You have to figure out yeast, inflammation, gastrointestinal stuff, visual stuff, auditory processing stuff, sensory processing stuff, food, diet, probiotics, homeopathy, supplements, herbs, sleep remedies, brain remedies, soul remedies (though I don't really believe that our souls need remedy; it just sounded like something that would strengthen my argument), gut remedies, schools, child care . . .

But the truth is that I know Barbara is right. I don't really believe all that defensive, rationalizing chatter that's triggered whenever someone tells me to stop acting like life is a race. It doesn't serve anyone that I become something like a pressure cooker. In my last talk with Barbara, she explained to me that I have lost my access to my own receptive mode. I have become a doer, operating with something like 70 percent of masculine energy, according to Barbara. That it is a challenge for a man to enter my world. I laughed when I heard that. And then I cried. Because I have never been interested in being a man. And then I spent some time observing myself to understand what I was doing and where I seemed to be going, hoping that just watching myself would help me find my way back to the life I wanted again. I tried to watch my actions, my holding on, my desperate attempts to figure everything out without judging any of it, without trying to change anything, and without freaking out. I tried to slow down enough to give myself more chances to be who I wanted to be, and who, deep down, I already was.

I know most of us learn new things best when we slow down. With boxing, for example, it's impossible to learn how to draw a powerful punch all the way from one's legs and pelvis and spine up through one's shoulders and arms without watching it and doing it in slow motion first. One has to step back, see someone else show it before trying it. When first trying it out, one has to move slowly, until it feels like a natural movement, until it transforms from an instruction, an idea, into becoming a muscle memory, something natural and instinctual.

The funny thing is, as much as my friends make fun of me for moving fast, I really enjoy the feeling of slowing down. Every time I do it, every time I meditate, for example, or take an extra breath before saying something and then feeling that there is enough space for me to decide that staying quiet is the better option, or take a yoga class, where I can't suddenly jump up and take care of something, or simply walk a little slower, I feel like I'm closer to myself.

Sometimes life forces us to slow down. The other day, as Lina and I drove out to North Salem after spending the weekend in New York City, I got a speeding ticket. I was already feeling a little overtaxed by my own internal dialogue about what I had to do and figure out that day. Maybe that's why I drove over 80 miles per hour rather than the designated 65.

"Do you know what the speed limit is?" the blond police officer asked me in a serious tone.

"65."

"You drove over 80 miles an hour."

"Yes."

I have pleaded with policemen in the past, and sometimes it's worked out well; sometimes it hasn't. But I was not in a pleading place and simply handed him my license and the registration and sat down to wait for my ticket. As I sat there, tears began to drip-drop down my cheeks. Soon, I was full-on crying, which I hadn't done for the past month, because I had simply felt too tired to cry. But now I suddenly had the energy to cry, and I felt how my whole system calmed down. The policeman, who noticed the tears, asked me if I felt that I was able to drive. I smiled inwardly. I was better able to drive now than I had been for a long time.

"Definitely," I responded and drove off. Lina, uncanny as she is without ever seeming deliberate about it, found Bob Dylan's "Shelter from the Storm" on my phone, and I had the opportunity to let some more tears cleanse and calm my system. Then Lina and I went to the house, had a NeuroMovement lesson as we always do, and drove up to Baxter Road for our daily hike. On the way there, I thought maybe I should just pay the ticket now, to get it over with. No, my inner judge told me, you would be taking away from Lina's hiking time. That would not be good for Lina. I watched my internal chatter about this dilemma and drove to the post office anyway.

Lina was in a splendid mood. She skipped into there like she owned the place. She was so comfortable that she decided to take her shoes off. She giggled, skipped, and looked around the dull post office with her eyes glittering, chuckling away. The post office lady looked at Lina and told me about her sixteen-year-old son.

"They are so much alike," she said. "My son skips around the house just like that."

The sweet office clerk told me about her son's struggles with his new high school, while helping me figuring out how to fill out the speeding ticket payment form. Before Lina and I left there, we tentatively decided to arrange a play date for Lina and Jason. It had been a good day for a ticket, and it reminded me that life isn't about judging this or that, having regrets about every other thing that happens to us, but rather welcoming everything, watching it all passing before our eyes and senses, knowing that none if it has very much at all to do with who we truly are.

It's funny how we are the most protected when we don't protect. The safest when we don't defend. The happiest when we don't reach for what we think will make us happy. The fullest when we let ourselves be empty. The readiest when we allow ourselves to relax, feel fully, breathe fully, let things happen, let things come and go. Our most protective shelter is whenever we are right out in the middle of the open, where wind and sun and rain and snow can touch us and move us and free us in a way that no thought pattern, no encouraging words, no defensive justification, no mind, no possession, no relationship, no position can ever do.

Lina teaches me so much about this. She is so free. When she loves someone, she shows it. No games. When she is happy, everyone in her world knows it. She isn't hung up on what's appropriate or inappropriate; she couldn't care less. Tales, Lina, and I went to a car dealership in Bridgeport, Connecticut, hoping to buy a truck. The transaction was taking a long time, and Lina got bored. It was hot in the office, because that particular November afternoon was colder than usual and the dealers had turned on a little heater in the room. Lina chuckled, and, sooner than anyone had a chance to blink or realize what just happened, she had pulled her shirt off and stood topless in the middle of the room. Sweet Tales jumped up and in front of Lina to shield her from the view of the two dealers. In a matter of seconds, I had pulled the shirt back on Lina and moved back onto the subject of the truck. Lina presents so many interesting, dramatic situations wherever she goes, one just has to learn how not to get caught up in any of it, in one's ego or in concerns and fears of what anyone else is going to think or do about this or that. Lina is so free that it's intolerable to be around her unless one frees oneself, too.

In spite of Lina doing much better, we still had a long way to go. Her progress was constantly interrupted by intense and ongoing OCD. In early January of 2018, Mary Coyle, our homeotoxicologist, and I decided to try another round of detox. She had been in contact with a homeopathy company in California that specializes in treating bacteria such as mycoplasma and strep. We wanted to see if we could get to the bottom of the mycoplasma dilemma, not just keeping it under control, but eliminating these vicious bacteria from her system altogether, never to have to deal with another flare-up again. It went well at first with all the preparatory drops. As soon as I started with the actual detox drops, Lina's ground began to shake. There were breakdowns. Screaming. Hitting. Hurting herself. I backed off and consulted Scott Huber. He saw that Lina's liver wasn't working effectively enough to process the toxins being flushed by the detox process. This is the ongoing dilemma in children damaged by toxins—the process of trying to eliminate toxins often triggers more challenges.

It was Monday. It seemed like Lina was back in the worst quarters. Tony got hit in the head in the middle of the night. I had been through enough of these phases and learned to move past them, but this time, as Lina and I were driving up to North Salem, I cried the whole way there. A lot about Lina is a gift. But the suffering, the anxiety-ridden OCD, the uncontainable emotion, the screaming and hitting and throwing, the dangerous situations that keep returning to our life, into our family, affecting her, all of us, and everyone around us, are difficult to understand and accept.

The next morning, as I was working on my computer upstairs, I heard Lina screaming downstairs. She was with Carla, and from the sound of it, the situation had quickly escalated. I ran downstairs and came in right after a big crash. Lina had just thrown a large brick of Himalayan salt across the kitchen in the direction of Carla, who had not been hit but was shaken. Lina calmed down quickly, but the event reminded me of the precariousness of our situation.

It had recently been a time of losses. Alison, who was teaching Lina two afternoons a week and providing Carla with school material and direction for the other three days, had come to a decision to quit. Of course, I wanted her to stay, but she felt that she had to move on, and that was that. No one can tell another person what to do.

I don't think it is about right or wrong. We are who we are. We go in the direction we think will serve us and our families the best, and along that path we find people who are heading in a similar direction. Someplace down the line, our paths diverge, or we realize they only crossed for a short while before separating again. Maybe later we end up in similar places. Maybe not. When Alison told me she was leaving, I felt confused and sad about it; the timing was challenging. Then I just dropped it. The blessing with Lina is that you really have to learn to move on. There is no time to cling. No time even to regret. The next thing happens, and then it seems like whatever happened is already in the past. And that is that.

There were more doors closing. After Alison left, I began looking for a music teacher. Music is essential to Lina. I was hoping to find someone whom had the ability to help her make her own music and express herself that way. A music teacher came by to evaluate whether he could help Lina sing and potentially play the piano. The man, who I'll call Marc, seemed softhearted and respectful, and still interested in Lina after she went from sitting and eating her breakfast eggs to a full-blown breakdown that involved not only deafening screaming, but her fist on my chest and a kick on the side of my hips. After Lina calmed down, Marc was still willing to work with Lina and offered to give me lessons, as well. After Marc had filled up the living room with his beautiful piano playing and deep-voice singing from *The Sound of Music,* which Lina eventually joined in with, we booked lessons for both me and Lina in South Salem the following Monday. Lina did indeed sing "Fool on the Hill" and a few other songs with Marc during her first official lesson, but then her OCD got the best of her, and a water bottle got spilled on Marc's couch. We left, feeling defeated. I cancelled my lesson and went back to the farm. The next morning, Marc wrote an email recommending that I contact an official organization with a licensed music therapist rather than continuing to work with him.

When life presents challenges, it's not the time to question things, to get bogged down, to stare at the obstacles. It's the time to rest in the trust that created the world. It's the time to know and experience the ultimate truth about who we are and to know, really know, that most of what we have learned to believe in as our true identity—our difficult experiences, our personality, our thoughts and feelings, our hopes and fears—is *not* who we really are. Our challenges help us to come home to our true self. Lina has helped me to find my way beyond all the surface stuff that does not matter one little bit.

Lina's difficulties continued. After an appointment with Mary Coyle, we learned that Lina most likely still was having seizures during her out-of-control breakdowns. Lina's attempts to push microbes like the mycoplasma bacteria and other bacteria and toxins out of her own system with the help of various homeopathic drops was not successful. It had turned into an autoimmune attack that led to Lina's recent out-of-control behavior and, as it turned out, seizures. We realized we had to go even slower with anything that would help Lina push toxins out of her system. It seemed like such a catch-22. These are complicated processes and I was trying to understand them, but I also felt there was no time. I was just trying to get through the day now. I was working with Tales on issues regarding the farm, and working with Carla on composing Lina's school days and keeping her safe and as happy and productive as possible during this difficult time. I had to cancel the overnight playdate with one of Lina's friends, because Lina was spending most of her awake time in a state of agitated OCD. Tales had found a nice older couple who wanted to donate some woodworking machines to our farm. They had a granddaughter with profound brain damage and were interested in looking into her being involved in the farm. Tales and I drove our "red trunk," as Lina lovingly refers to the truck, to pick up the machines. On the way there, Tales discussed ideas for making North Salem accessible. I looked at Tales. His face was beaming with enthusiasm, and he was ready to delve into the next project at the farm.

"It's a great idea, for sure, Tales, though we are not there yet. You know, Lina is a mess and it's kind of like your house is on fire and you go and send invitations to your neighbors for your upcoming housewarming party. We aren't really in a position to spend months or more to make North Salem accessible for the child in a wheelchair that we have not even met yet."

The thoughts of how to best help Lina, while at the same time keeping my own head above water, were slowly taking shape. I knew North Salem was a good thing. And it was wonderful to have Tales and Carla with us there. All of that was good.

Then there was the day, a month or so after Alison left, when Carla and Tales let me know that they would move out in three weeks. Carla had gotten a very promising job offer within the area of design, her great passion.

I felt sad for Lina's sake. I had so much wanted for her to have a community. A place in the world where she would be surrounded by love and understanding. An easy place where she could be who she was without having to hold back. But now it was just us again. Me, Lina, and occasionally Elsa. I wasn't sure whether the best thing would be to keep trying or let it go.

CHAPTER NINE

A New Direction

O NE MONDAY MORNING at the end of February, as Lina and I drove up from the city to North Salem to start Lina's school week, I realized that I had failed to communicate with Tony all the things I had learned from our latest tests and the consultation with Mary Coyle about Lina's recent seizures. I called him up and described the findings and the latest approach to Lina's recovery. He responded in the same way as he has done so many times before when I was trying to account for my latest idea about what we needed to do to promote Lina's recovery.

"Helena, the thing is, every doctor, everyone that we consult about Lina is going to say different things. We have to find time to do our own research. You don't have that time now because you are trying to be Lina's case worker, her pharmacist, her teacher, the farmer . . ."

"I will back off when Lina is feeling better," I said in my usual stubborn manner.

"It's just that when you are all those things for Lina, you don't have time to think about the bigger picture. You don't have time to do the research that would ultimately help Lina."

Like so many tiresome times before, I was about to start trying to convince Tony that I could do that too, that it wouldn't be a problem, but I realized it just wasn't so. He was right. I didn't have time now to do anything but try to get us all through the day. There wasn't, magically, some incredible brain doctor stepping forth in our lives, knowing what was wrong with Lina. We would never find the solution to Lina's difficulties if we didn't have time to sit down and study all the processes that were going wrong in Lina's nervous system. I thought about North Salem. I thought about how well everything had been going for the first five months and how, recently, everything was falling apart again. How would I be able to do all this and still find the right people to help Lina with her inflammation, her mycoplasma bacteria, her viral issues, the mercury that was still in her system, the auto-immune attacks that again caused the seizures that she was now back in the trenches of? I thought about my hopes for the North Salem farm, my wish to finish what I started, the way I was used to doing things. It was such a wonderful idea. I had been working so hard to make it all happen. The farm was so perfect for this purpose, so ready to be a blessing for many. But all of this was ultimately for Lina and Elsa. They were my first responsibility. If Lina was still suffering and I didn't have the time I needed to figure out how I could help her, what was the point? Maybe each one of the obstacles that had piled up in front of me was a way to help me shift direction? I sat quiet for a couple of minutes, listening to Tony's calm voice, describing how my doing everything with Lina wasn't the best way to help her. How sometimes, taking a step back can be the most helpful thing you can do for another person. As I listened to his voice and watched my own habitual objections and reactions to his words, I realized there was something in what he was saying that was good. There was the idea that Lina and Elsa were our priority, that nothing else was more important than them right now. There was the fact that we have to do research. We have to get Lina back; we could not give up on her now and settle. There was the thought that somewhere, out there, was a solution. We just had to find it. Finding it would take research. Research would take time. I didn't have any time. I had to find time. In less than a couple of minutes, I decided to put North Salem Movement and Learning Center on hold and saw a potential solution.

I proposed something I had dismissed in the past as too impractical when we lived in the city. I proposed that, for the time being, we send Lina to Otto Specht, a private Waldorf school for special needs kids. It was in Rockland county, an hour away from North Salem and a little less than an hour from the city. But Lina would have friends, and I would have time for research. We could get her back. They have cows and gardens at Otto Specht, too. It's all natural and no Wi-Fi there. Lina would love it.

Tony liked the idea. Lina, on the other hand, wanted to put the music back on, was tired of us talking, started squirming, and was soon screaming on top of her lungs. Tony said something about how, during the current circumstances, while we are pretty tough, it would be a bit challenging to try to figure out autoimmune processes and brain inflammation. While he spoke,

Lina threw a water bottle from the backseat in my direction, illustrating the point beautifully. I laughed, relieved that we seemed to be off in a new direction. And that was that. I emailed the director at Otto Specht the next day.

A couple weeks later, on a Monday in late March, Lina and I visited Otto Specht, in Chestnut Ridge, New York. Lina was not yet ready to walk into the classroom with five other children, all around the same age or slightly younger than she. Lina stood in the hallway of the oval-shaped school building up on a hill, usually referred to as the auditorium, with beautiful wooden doors and a large spiral staircase in the entrance, and eventually had her morning snack in the room next to where the children were sitting. After a walk on forest paths, along a small brook, up a steep hill to where one of the school's multiple greenhouses were located, the whole group walked back to the auditorium. It was one of the first warm days of spring, and we all had our lunch outside, around a round wooden table handmade by a student's father. By lunchtime, Lina had warmed up to the group and ate her chicken legs and sauerkraut with a big smile on her face. She knew one of the teachers who had worked at Atlas with her in the past and two of the five children, who had both been students at Atlas prior to coming to Otto Specht. The teachers were easygoing and friendly, and having lunch with them felt like sitting around with a bunch of girlfriends. Every Thursday was hike day, when kids of all ages, and with all kinds of special needs, went hiking together with their teachers. The hike would lead through wooded paths across big fields and hills and across brooks and swamps.

One of those Thursdays, after Lina became a student, Elsa, who had her spring break, came along, as well. Soon, she was walking way ahead of Lina and me and most others in the group of teachers and children that were on the hike, chatting away with a boy from a different class. During lunch, sitting around on tree stumps and rocks, Lina seemed happy and at peace. Elsa sat by the trunk of a large tree, carving wood with Mrs. Chin and three of the boys from a different class. An older boy, whom Lina knew from Atlas, was conversing with one of the art teachers about his difficulties to stop using profanity. Lina listened in on the conversation, giggling as she recognized that the young man was enjoying the subtle reactions he got from the teacher when he occasionally failed the task of not using profanity. All the teachers treated me like an old friend. We had finally found the educational home for Lina that we had been looking for. I wondered why I hadn't thought about this before trying to create something that was already here.

There were greenhouses. A farm with cows and sheep and chickens and geese. Threefold Café, where some of the Otto Specht students had opportunities to try out their first jobs. There was a beautiful retirement home on the campus, all part of the larger Rudolf Steiner Fellowship Program. The school welcomed children on and off the spectrum with sensory, social, emotional, and cognitive challenges, in small, individualized settings, using a curriculum that promotes art, music, and movement, as well as lots of grounding, practical work including animal care, gardening, weaving, painting, and woodworking. Lina and I visited a few more times, for another hike, a few classroom activities, some greenhouse work, and lunches. But all along, I had no doubt this was the right thing for Lina. Here was the community I knew she wanted and needed. In spite of what everyone says about autism, it's not something that makes someone disinterested in social connection. Lina is a deeply social human being. She connects easily with whoever gives her the time of day, and sometimes even when someone doesn't. The fact that we weren't able to create a community in North Salem at this time had more to do with me than with her. I am not a deeply social person. I like to spend time alone. Not all the time, but a substantial amount of time every day, if possible. I feel very different about the time I spend with Lina. She doesn't talk as much as other people. She doesn't have to nurture her ego. She has a rich inner life that doesn't seek confirmation on the outside. I find it easier to be with her than with most other people. There is a spaciousness around her that is hard to come by with most people. A quiet understanding that goes way beyond words, explanations, and rationalizations. A sense of humor and a kind of perspective that can only exist in a truly egoless person.

That's another thing about Otto Specht. Being around trees and cows, hiking through the woods, working with vegetables and flowers, creating art out of natural materials, rocks, driftwood, naturally hand-colored wool, and eating organic foods does something to the children here. It evokes their natural gentleness that comes from Mother Earth herself; calm, soft, rhythmical days, brought on by closeness to Earth's own rhythm, so different from the noisy, hectic, tense, desperate, artificial rhythm of the city.

Lina's teacher seemed not only open to, but actively interested in, Lina's RPM experiences and in the possibility of offering RPM as part of the school day. I had been discussing this with other mothers in Lina's class as well as parents planning to send their children to Otto Specht. The next time I ran into Jeanette, the director of the Otto Specht school, in the Threefold Café next to her office, she was already on board with bringing RPM to Otto Specht. Jeanette's openness to whatever seemed helpful to some of the children and her "why not?" attitude were so refreshing and hopeful. The same "why not?" mindset inspired one of the Otto

Specht teachers to bring his horse, Odis, to the farm to provide the kids with horse therapy. It was as if everything good that I had hoped to give to Lina, the horseback riding, the RPM, the natural environment, were coming together in this one special place.

After a couple of weeks of Lina getting used to her new school with me by her side, it was time for me to let Lina try her own wings. I suddenly had time to focus on Lina from a different perspective and implement some of my research.

I started her on a progesterone cream to help stabilize her blood sugar, in combination with a new meal plan recommended by Dr. Michael Platt that allowed an even influx of the right kind of sugar (mostly from green vegetables) to the brain. The changes had significant and immediate results. Lina was calmer and more balanced and centered than she had been in months. She seemed increasingly in sync with herself.

We continued our outside RPM lessons with Jane. When asked what Lina wanted to study, she wrote "God." At one point, discussing Buddhism, she wrote:

"Wisdom is easy when someone really reaches for it." For her, it seems so obvious.

When Jane presented a lesson about rare books, Lina humored her young teacher for a little bit by adding her perspective on rare books from 1100 to 1953 as "something real beautiful" but then asked to change the subject. She wanted to talk about music. She volunteered that she is "not into rap," and that "no one is as cool as Rihanna." Jane played a song by Drake. I apologetically blurted out that I like Drake. I felt apologetic about it, because however much I try to ignore it, I know he is not the nicest to women. But I didn't say that. Instead, Jane asked Lina what she thought of him. "He is too emotional," Lina wrote and added, "He is not a feminist." So true.

CHAPTER TEN

Self-Compassion

WHEN YOU HAVE a child with challenges as severe and undeniable as Lina's, you look for healing modalities wherever you can find them, trying everything under the sun, leaving no stone unturned, being willing to believe any, however outrageous-sounding, idea that might help. You may look at me and see someone who's about to go off the deep end. Or if you are kind and understanding, you may consider me open-minded or even brave. But if you are me—watching Lina scream louder than the most impressive primal screams, helplessly watching her body writhe in pain, biting and punching herself or someone nearby, crying desperately and not being able to find the words to describe what she is feeling—whether I am brave or insane doesn't matter much. What I thought yesterday has no bearing on what I'm thinking today. I am willing to abandon any concept, any teaching, any supplement, any living situation, any profession, anything, in favor of something that would be more helpful to Lina and Elsa. What I'm feeling about my own life or where I am with myself seems so ridiculously irrelevant in the face of Lina's struggle.

Only it isn't.

Autism is the biggest paradox that I have ever come across. In my life with Lina, I have found happiness that I didn't know existed. And I have felt sorrow, grief, and terror in watching my daughter fall apart, over and over, in such violent, desperate, and dangerous ways that I will never be able to explain to anyone else no matter how hard I try, unless they have had similar experiences.

Lina has taught me how to live in more unconditional ways, less dependent on circumstances. To know that everything is perfect the way it is, in spite of the fact that life sometimes appears apocalyptic. That laughing and crying are sister and brother. That Lina is somehow intact in the middle of every-thing. And that I am, too.

So why do I say that there is nothing to fix, nothing to heal, nothing to alter, while at the same time I don't ever stop search-ing for healing for Lina? I don't know. I can't explain it. It's the autism contradiction. But it's beyond autism. I have found it to be one of the many incomprehensible contradictions in life and living in general.

Somewhere in between those seemingly oppositional thoughts, I found myself on a plane to New Mexico, to seek healing for myself from an indigenous Navajo shaman who had a lot of experience of the kind of heavy, ancestral baggage I had lugged around for most of my life.

Only the plane wouldn't leave. There was something wrong with it. Hours went by before they could establish that the plane was fit for flying. Finally, we were in the air. In Dallas, though, we were not only late for the connecting flight, but the plane to Albuquerque, where I was going, was cancelled. So as not to risk being late to my healing, I booked a flight to Phoenix. That plane wouldn't take off, either. It was something about the runway, that it was very busy and our plane had been slightly late so now there was no space for it to take off. The suspense continued. We eventually did fly, but now came the question of whether we would make it in time for the connecting flight in Phoenix, which we magically did. While we made it there in time, though, the crew was missing. Finally, the slightly stressed-out, skinny young man at the boarding desk triumphantly announced that the crew was on the way! Then the young man reluctantly grabbed the microphone again (I can only imagine his sweaty palms) to announce that, while they had indeed located the crew, the captain was nowhere to be found! I laughed out loud; it just seemed so funny. By the time I'd landed in Albuquerque after my all-day flight adventure, I was just happy to be there, on my way to meet with the Navajo people. I was at least trying to show up for myself, and that was good enough for me.

My friend Rupert, of the Horse Boy project, was waiting patiently for me at the airport. He was the one who had told me about the Navajos and the shaman, Chee, or Blue Horse as he is referred to by the Navajo people. It was good to have a friend by my side. Charles, who is Blue Horse's assistant and author of *Spirit Land: The Peyote Diaries of Charles Langley*, had helped me set everything up with Blue Horse. Normally he attended the healings; this time, however, he had a conference to go to with his wife. Charles had cautioned me not to wander around

Albuquerque or Gallup by myself, since both towns had high crime rates. I knew I would be protected and was not even the slightest bit conflicted about whether to go or not, but when Rupert, or Rufus, as Blue Horse insisted on calling him, decided to come along, I was very happy. We didn't get to our hotel in the outskirts of Gallup until 12:30 a.m. We got our herbal teas from the reception area downstairs and went off to sleep. The next day would be a long day, and we wanted to be ready for it.

I woke up early, did my yoga, and ate as many scrambled eggs and turkey patties that I could manage to pack in. I am a functionalist when it comes to healing, and I am also a functionalist when it comes to food. Most of what I eat is just fuel, what I know my body needs at any given time. In between, I eat for pleasure, but my main diet is more about getting the right, and enough, energy. This morning was all about quantity. When that job was completed, we filled our cups with tea and coffee and jumped in the car.

Rupert can talk. He is also a really good listener. We missed our exit and had to find our way back to route I-40. Eventually we got off the main highway and drove up the right mountain. The sun was gliding up higher in the cloudless sky; everything was empty, there was just sand, bushes, wild sage, and red mountains as far as the eye could see. I felt so calm and happy. This was a day I had been waiting for my whole life. We stopped to pee, my friend on one side of the road, I on the other. When I stood up from behind the little scraggly bush I had been hiding behind, Rupert was already by the car, smiling back over at me. I took a step, and for a reason I can't explain, I simply fell down into a patch of thorny sage bushes. It must have looked ridiculous and I laughed, happy that life always had a way of putting a humorous spin on things. We came to a farm with two small, skinny dogs and some sheep. A woman eventually came out from a tiny wooden house to see what we were doing on her land and pointed us in the direction of Blue Horse's house. We had to get out on the main road again and drive around a few smaller back roads.

Blue Horse's house was only slightly bigger than his neighbor's. He had dogs as well, three of them, freely roaming around the driveway in front of the house, cautiously checking us out as we parked under a tree not far from the house. About thirty yards below the house, but still up on a hill with a stunning view in almost every direction, a fire was already sending smoke up toward the sky. In front of the fireplace was a little shed. Baa, Blue Horse's wife, his nephew, and his grandson were in the house as we knocked and came in to introduce ourselves. Baa told us Blue Horse was already down by the sweat lodge. As we got there, I realized the sweat lodge was built inside the little shed. It filled up most of the inside of the shed, built like an igloo, insulated with thick blankets rather than ice and with a frame of sturdy but bendable wooden branches. I eventually learned that the branches were arranged in ways that represented the twelve months, the four directions, and the healing elements trusted by the Navajos to be part of every ceremony: the rocks, the fire, the water.

I stood outside the shed next to the fire and looked out at the red mountains that stretched out everywhere in front of me. I felt the warmth of the sun and the wind and the smoke from the fire on my skin and knew this was the best thing that I had done for a long time. I didn't worry about whether it would work or not. The thought, honestly, did not even occur to me. Sometimes you just know. It's not about feeling this way or that way. It's not about figuring it out cognitively in one's head. It's not because someone else did it and it worked or that someone convinced you that it would. I just knew as soon as we walked down to the sweat lodge that I was at the right place at the perfect time. That my life would be a little bit different from then on. I didn't know how that would be. I just knew it would.

We walked into the shed where Blue Horse was sitting on a white plastic chair next to the newly built sweat lodge. He looked old and tired. But there was no question from the way his eyes followed us as we walked into the shed that he was a fully seeing, fully aware, acutely observant individual. He asked us about our trip, and I mumbled something about it but didn't want to introduce any ideas about obstacles and challenges. We were here and that was all that mattered. We sat around talking for a little while, and I showed Blue Horse pictures of Lina and Elsa. He looked at them quietly and then said, "It's very green where you live."

It was clear that Blue Horse liked to make jokes. At one point he turned around to the wall behind him and picked up a piece of wood with a handle that was hanging behind him.

"Board of Ed," he said, smiling the half toothless grin that I was soon quite enthralled by, and gesturing with the board how it could be used for spanking disobedient children. Then he turned to me and said:

"Maybe you'll become a medicine woman."

I didn't say anything.

"Who is your clan?" Blue Horse continued, looking right at me as if my answer to this one would be important.

"Um, well, I have just a little bit of contact with my clan," I said apologetically and held up my thumb and index finger with a tiny space in between them.

"You have to know your clan," Blue Horse muttered half to himself, half to me.

I thought about the shamans up in the northern parts of Sweden and my lame attempts to contact them and set up some kind of communication, a meeting even. I thought about what Malidoma, the shaman who had done divinations a couple of years ago for Lina, Tony, and me, had said about how important it would be to go there, to take the girls to Sweden, and have them know about my northern magic people. I had my own magic when I was a little girl, running around in the woods, talking to trees, elves, and trolls. That was home for me and freedom from the things I couldn't understand and integrate in my early life. I knew he was right and thought to myself that this may be the beginning of a different kind of journey, a deeper, richer, and more integrated one.

Then, before I had a chance to respond, Blue Horse talked about his injured knee. He had been a horse man, just like Rupert, before this injury. He had fallen under a horse while chasing bulls, and his knee was still bothering him. From reading *The Spirit Land*, I knew Blue Horse has healed anything from cancer to severe eczema to every debilitating pain known to man, dangerous blood clots, tracheotomies, suicidality, loss of mobility, loss of speech, and many other challenges among Navajos, as well as nonnatives. At some point, Rupert went to go get something from the car. As soon as he was outside of the cabin, Blue Horse quickly turned to me, leaning closer so no one else should hear him:

"So, can you tell me again what you want help with?"

I had already written to Blue Horse's assistant, Charles, about why I had wanted to come, and Charles had already talked with Blue Horse about it. He had told Charles that it wouldn't be easy and that he would bring in another shaman to assist in the healing. The last thing I wanted to do was to reinforce negative stuff in my life by telling and retelling stories about it. But I guess he wanted to hear directly from me.

"I have a lot of fear and panic; I feel it right here." I pointed to the middle of my chest. "I have felt it for most of my life, since I was a little girl, but it's reinforced by my oldest daughter's challenges. It's a kind of terror. I just want to be free from it."

"Ok, good. I will do what I can. I can't guarantee anything, but I will try to take it away."

I thanked him.

We all sat around talking about this or that while Blue Horse's nephew and his grandson prepared the sage bouquet that would be used for splashing sage water on the hot rocks as well as on everyone inside the sweat lodge. The two young men kept the fire right outside the shed going. There were a number of rocks in the middle of the fire. Eventually, the bigger of the two, the nephew, took a fork to shovel out one of the hot stones that was in the fire and placed it inside the sweat lodge. He brought a few more of those rocks into the lodge before Blue Horse gestured for us all to go inside. We had to crawl in there on all fours, including Blue Horse with his bad knee, and took our seats as he instructed us. There were four other shamans inside with us. Then Blue Horse's nephew and grandson, as well as one of the other shaman's two children, a woman and mother of four children, her little brother, and a young man in his twenties showed up. The little tent was filled to the brim. Blue Horse's wife, Baa, who was no longer healthy enough to participate inside the sweat lodge, sat on a chair outside, holding Blue Horse's sacred feather. She too was a medicine woman, and while I didn't see much of her during our day with the Navajos, her gentle demeanor and almost weary awareness didn't pass me by. I had the distinct feeling that she had seen most of what there is to see by the human eye. But she didn't seem the type to make up unnecessary stories about it in her own mind. She just struck me as one of those people who shrugged at almost anything and kept on keeping on.

Inside the sweat lodge, the air grew thick and hot. The nephew brought yet another couple of hot rocks, and Blue Horse threw water from a bucket by splashing the tied-up bundle of sage onto the rocks. There were a few different kinds of sage in the water too, and the smoke smelled fresh and sweet from the wild herbs. The entrance was sealed with thick blankets, and soon sweat was pouring down my face and arms and every other body part of everyone inside the lodge. Blue Horse had told me to scream if I needed to get out, but not once during the four rounds of sweat, an hour or two each, with chanting, praying, singing, and eventually Blue Horse blowing in his pipe to call for what he was going to remove inside of me, did I have the impulse to leave or even ask anyone to remove the blanket as to let some air in. I felt like I had finally come home. I sang along as well as I could in the spirited chanting and made up a song of my own about Lina, sleeping peacefully under the moon and playing joyfully under the sun. I tried my best to send out some prayers on my own behalf, as Blue Horse instructed me to while someone was drumming, and realized how praying for myself is something I need to practice. I watched Blue Horse pull out some black, nasty-looking liquid stuff from my neck. I have no idea what that was about. All I know is that whatever happened after this healing, my life would be different from this moment on. I stretched out my arms toward the fire and licked up every drop of sage water that someone splashed on my face. I listened to every word, every chant, and witnessed my beautiful friend Rupert sing with his whole heart songs about ships and crops, and pray about love and compassion and healing for all of us. I felt such deep love for everyone in there, and especially for Blue

Horse, for going through this rigorous procedure, year in and year out, to help heal not only his own people, but the very people who had disrespected and invaded and exploited him, who had washed his mouth with soap when as a child he spoke the Navajo language in the school run by white people that he was forced to attend.

Time stood still. Everything was as it should be. The hot air, the smoke from the rocks, the sweet smell of the sacred sage water, the sun and the red mountains outside, the vast, quiet space, the dry orange sand, the fire outside the shed, the half-wild dogs running around the property watching everything from a distance. I didn't think about anything or anyone else. Nothing beyond being in that place was important. Nothing but the smoke, the heat, the fire, the water, and the sacred herbs were of any importance to me. I sat there in that hot circle, allowing everything to happen according to the traditional ancient wisdom of the indigenous Navajo people who had learned to listen beyond Wi-Fi, TV, and alarmist newscasters. Who understood what the sun and the moon and the stars were communicating; who could look into the fire and see what they needed to see about whoever was trusting them for healing; who had learned how to trust themselves and their power, because it was aligned with the power of Mother Earth and the universe.

And when it was all over, as Rupert and I were sitting on a log right outside the shed, watching the evening sun slowly beginning its journey down toward the red mountains far away to the west, I felt an emptiness that left me open to everything around me. An emptiness that had no preference. A space that wasn't trying to dictate or predict or maneuver or manipulate what was going to happen next. A vastness that feared nothing.

Later, back home in the Northeast, with life and its challenges surfacing as usual, I began to see that the biggest insight from my visit with Blue Horse and his family was that I needed to learn how to treat myself better. I also needed to pray for myself. Prayer is one of the ways that I have learned to love and pay attention to the people in my life. I have an altar at home in the city with symbols for my spiritual teachers and guides, my ancestors, the Indian commission (people like Blue Horse), my guardian angel, my protective animals. I have stones for my children and my close friends, which I use when thinking about them and sending love and healing to them. But as I got home, I realized I wanted to add a stone for myself. I wanted to learn how to pay more attention to myself and send love and blessings in my own direction. It somehow felt like an uphill process. And it seemed a bit tragicomic that at almost fifty-three years old, having worked as a psychoanalyst for decades and having prayed for most of my life, I just now figured out that I had to learn how to really pay attention to, and appreciate, myself. I felt that a lot was dependent on whether I would be willing to do that, that things couldn't fully develop and heal unless I was able to show myself the love that I was born to experience in the same way as we are all born to feel and know it. Being away from that pure self-compassion and appreciation is like living in the shadow of one's own life. And when we discover ourselves, our own internal beauty, and learn to pray for ourselves or honor ourselves in whatever way comes naturally to us, the shadow fades away in the light; darkness cannot touch us; we are no longer lonely; we are not living in fear. We are free, connected to God and the universe. The trip to the Navajos was the beginning of my understanding that I was as intact, beautiful, and full of love as anything and anyone can be. And because of that, I had nothing to be afraid of. Nothing, not even my own fear. All I had to do was to keep accepting that I had been entrusted to be here on this planet with my wonderful two girls, doing the best I can to keep them happy and safe, going to bed each night and waking up each day counting my blessings. Or, as Blue Horse would put it, "Just keep on moving; go live your life." And when difficult situations arise, to approach them in the most sincere and compassionate way possible.

One sunny July morning, as I was driving Lina to camp at Otto Specht, Lina started shouting and moving around in that jerky, agitated way that I recognized as the almost inevitable precursor to bigger breakdowns. There was a lot of tension in her legs, and I braced myself. Then I suddenly felt tired of the fear, tired of the precariousness of trying to drive safely with Lina falling apart in the backseat. I pulled off the road. I turned the car off.

"Lina, if you fall apart in the car like this, we won't be able to drive together. This whole thing, the freedom that we have driving around everywhere, to school, to the house, to Jane, to wherever we need to go, we won't have anymore. It's not because I'm punishing you or because you're bad for falling apart, it's because it's not safe. Not for you and not for me, either."

Lina looked at me. She stopped screaming. Tension faded away from her body, and her face got soft.

"I don't want to live in fear that something will happen to us, that we'll crash, that you'll kick me from behind. You can scream and fall apart at any other point, just not when we're driving. I am telling you, and I know this is very hard for you to control, trust me, I get that, but we have no choice."

Then we drove to camp. Lina was calm and mellow the rest of that day and all of the following day. I didn't really know what to make of it. The one thing I had noticed after I came back from the Navajos was that people around me, including the super and the managing agent for the building we live in on the Upper West Side, seemed to be able to listen to me and empathize even when I got upset and called them out on things. Maybe this was true for Lina, too? Maybe I was able to communicate how I felt about things more fully, so she had an easier time responding to it? Maybe she somehow picked up on my increasing sense of self-compassion and heard me in a different way as I was talking to her about my own feelings, my own need to keep myself safe? We drove the hour and a half from Lina's camp at Otto Specht in Spring Valley, New York, to Jane's office at Cadman's Plaza in Brooklyn without a single OCD episode, not even a small one.

At Jane's office Lina just calmly walked in, ready to work. Jane talked about verbs, adverbs, pronouns, and nouns, and Lina, moderately interested, rattled off various examples of each. "Who had ever taught her that?" I wondered. After a little more of the grammar lesson, Lina visibly and audibly restless and "ready to leave and go to the blue car," Jane said okay, let's pick another lesson. Jane couldn't possibly have known that Rupert had just handed me Neil Gaiman's *Norse Mythology*, as his big brotherly way of reminding me to start connecting with my ancestor's history. I had even prepared a Norse Myth RPM lesson for Lina about Odin and Thor that I just hadn't carried out yet. When Jane said let's talk about the Northern Myths, I was very happy. Jane told a funny story about the thunderous Thor and his beautiful wife Safi and the deviant Loki, who somehow inevitably got himself and his fellow giants into trouble. When the lesson was done, Jane moved on to the last minutes of the session, allowing for a little more personal expression, should Lina feel up for it.

"Lina, if you were to write a Norse story, who would the main character be? Would it be a warrior like Thor or someone deviant like Loki or some other god?"

"Hero," Lina spelled out, as she looked over at me and smiled.

"Okay, so it would be about a hero? Anything else you'd like to say about that? Who is the hero?"

"Mom, a Norse hero," Lina wrote out.

"I see. And what would this story about Mom be about?" Jane asked, keeping her tone casual as not to pressure Lina to express more that she was ready for.

"The journey of helping me," Lina wrote, and then before Jane had a chance to ask anything else, Lina spelled out, "I'm not so sure I can."

"I believe you can, Lina. And I will help you. If you want to write about this journey, I know you can do it."

Lina looked so bright and centered for the rest of that day, and the next day, too. As always after Lina's RPM lessons, it was like she had gotten two inches taller, having expressed herself in a way that was faithful to her own internal thought process. Jane and RPM was Lina's occasional opportunity out of the autism maze of confusion, disarray, OCD, panic, misunderstandings, body betrayal, and humiliation. Our children on the spectrum have a way of leading us to our own darkest places. We can drown there, suffocate, be crushed by our own imperfection, or we can meet our children and ourselves in this place of no escape with forgiveness and self-compassion.

Lina and I left Lina's camp at Otto Specht. There was a gentle summer rain, and a murmuring thunder in the distance. The sky was dark gray. As I was waiting for Lina's day to end, I had gone to Target and bought a new rug for our city apartment. It was rolled up, and I jammed it into the corner of the backseat opposite Lina's seat. As Lina noticed the rug, she asked for it to be moved someplace else. I took the carpet out in the rain and pushed it down on the seat next to me in the front of the car. Part of it was leaning over toward me, but I thought to myself, if that's what will save the day, it's a small price to pay. Lina wasn't convinced. She started to raise her voice and tried to push it farther in my direction; the carpet was now partly hovering over the console shift. I tried to explain myself to Lina, but OCD was already running away with her, and there was absolutely nothing I could say to redirect her. Nothing. I knew that full well. And yet I felt like I could make it work, find a quick solution, move on, without having to go through the whole episode. I pulled over, got out of the car, and moved the carpet back to the far corner in the backseat, pressed it up along the side door and back window, all the while trying to explain to Lina how this was the only possible solution. Lina wasn't having it. It was not a solution that helped calm her down. She was screaming now and grabbed the carpet and started to try to rip it apart, as if it had been an enemy in a life-threatening battle. I watched as Lina tore the plastic off the rolled-up carpet, hitting it with her arms and legs and feet, screaming, crying. She looked like a trapped animal, unable to allow herself to be talked down from whatever panic she experienced. I started to feel my own tension welling up inside of me. My mind flooded with doubts about the kind of life we had where it was impossible to do something as seemingly simple as putting a rolled-up carpet in a corner of our car. Her deafening screams and agony touched something deep inside of me. We were now both in panic. I closed the door, watching Lina fight the beast that was just a carpet and watched my own agony swell inside of me. Lina was now trying to reach for something in the front seat. I had my computer, my phone, and some glass bottles, a lot of things that not only could be destroyed but might hurt her, too. Still in panic, I went back into the car. Lina's relentless rage continued. With all my clarity and centered awareness evaporated somewhere outside the car, far away, my voice became louder by the second. Now both of us were yelling and screaming about where the carpet should be and how wrong everything was. If it hadn't been so heartbreaking, it would have been funny. But it wasn't even the slightest bit funny. At one point, Lina stopped fighting the carpet and looked at me with big eyes, suddenly noticing that she wasn't the only one losing it. Her voice dropped down to regular tone. Mine was nowhere near normal.

"Calm down," she said.

"WE CAN'T HAVE THIS KIND OF LIFE, LINA, WHERE WE CAN'T DO ANYTHING WITHOUT IT TURNING INTO A BIG HELLISH SCENE! I JUST DON'T WANT TO BE THIS TRAPPED! YOU HAVE TO HELP ME, BABY, YOU GOTTA FIND IT, COME BACK TO ME, I AM JUST SO TIRED SO DEEPLY FUCKING TIRED, I JUST CAN'T DO THIS ON THIS DAMN LEVEL ANYMORE! CAN YOU HEAR ME?"

"Calm down," she said, again.

It was a very appropriate request. Had I not been so beside myself, I would have been happy for Lina that her brain somehow in that moment allowed her to say something that wasn't the opposite of what she was thinking, because that seemed to be the frustrating case for her most of the time. When she wanted to say, "open," she would say, "close." When she wanted to say, "go to the country," out came "go to the city." Instead of "me," it would be "you." But in this moment of clarity, Lina was able to tell me to "calm down." I cried for most of the way back to the city. Lina listened quietly to my sad ramblings. At some point I regained enough self-control to ask Lina how she was feeling.

"Happy."

I just looked at her in the rearview mirror. She was staring out the window but felt my gaze and looked back at me.

"Upset," she self-corrected.

"I get it, Lina. I am so sorry. The very last thing I want to do is to go off on you when you are in the middle of a panic. I know you really wouldn't be there if you could help it. Will you forgive me?" I asked and reached my hand back to give a low high five if she was willing.

"Yeah," she said without any hesitation and softly slapped my hand.

"Thank you, Lina. Love you so so much."

"So so so much," she reiterated.

"Is there anything else you would like to try to say, Lina?"

"Go to the doctor."

"You mean Scott Huber?"

"Yeah, take the blue car to Scott Huber."

"Anything else you think may be helpful to you?"

"Go to the white house. Swim in the pool."

I knew she was always doing better these days up at the house in North Salem. We were spending most of our time outside there, and outside was always easier for Lina than being indoors. In one of Lina's recent RPM lessons, after she had gotten loud and out of control, she explained this further. "Sorry, inside I get lots of OCD," she had spelled out and had also explained—in a way that revealed that she had full awareness of her condition and her challenges—how some "stories might trigger me."

I don't know what it was about the carpet that triggered Lina. But as we drove back home, Lina, uncharacteristically, didn't want to listen to any music. She just sat there, quietly. During the last part of our car ride, right before getting home, Lina suddenly grabbed the phone and started to browse through Spotify. She settled on Pharrell Williams's "Just a Cloud Away," from the movie *Despicable Me 2*.

As we got to the part of the song about "So what, you blown a fuse . . . ," a little sweet smile spread across Lina's beautiful face. She looked over at me. If eyes could talk, and I think they can a thousand times more than words, there she was, my teenage girl, trying to comfort me and tell me everything was alright, the day could change and sunshine wasn't as far away as it seemed. The next day, on the way to camp, after we had dropped off Elsa at her camp, I turned to Lina and said:

"Hey, Lina, I just want to say something about what happened yesterday, cool?"

"Yeah."

"You know, I was thinking about how the last thing I want to do is to lose it when you need me the most. I so much want to be helpful to you particularly when you're having a rough time. And when I can't I feel so terrible. I have to try to forgive myself. I know you already have. But maybe that's what you're feeling, too? That you don't want to lose it, and maybe particularly not with me, but you just can't help it?

"Yeah."

"But I know we are both just doing the best we can. And that has to be good enough. Anyway, that's all I had to say."

"That was all," Lina underlined, as if to make sure this difficult topic would be over and done with by now.

I think self-compassion, self-love, self-care, and self-forgiveness are particularly challenging notions for parents with children with severe challenges. In trying to help our children through their painful moments, we are reminded of our own deepest, darkest places, while at the same time, we take on our children's suffering. We take their shadow, or rather, the shadow we perceive around them. We fear that their suffering will be in the way of them being loved. We make ourselves the troubled ones, the unloved ones, the fearful ones so as to try to protect them from the possibility that their suffering keeps love and peace and compassion out of their reach. It doesn't make much sense, and it's not one of the most helpful things we do for our children. Helpful or not, I see it, not just in myself, but in many other special needs mothers and some fathers. I think we need to figure out how to find our own permission to stop doing that. We need to open our eyes and see our own love and beauty, in the middle of our imperfect ways. We need to learn to acknowledge that the way we want to care for our children, and the love we give to them, is how God wants to love us. When we figure this out, we can finally see that, like our children, we have been free all along, worthy of love, worthy of compassion and forgiveness, worthy of everything that life offers, and that this is true for every other living being on the planet.

Epilogue

"All language is a longing for home . . ."

—RUMI

A COUPLE OF days later, Lina and I sat around on our thick, bright red-green-and-blue blanket out in the grass on our North Salem farm, having dinner. She was so happy. She had been to school earlier that day. Seen her friends. Done her school work, had a life, had interactions with multiple people, just the way her heart desired. And now we were here, in the soft evening sun, eating kale chips and chicken cutlets dipped in egg and almond flour and fried in coconut oil. Everything was perfect, everything was still. Lina smiled as she chowed down one cutlet after the next. Suddenly she stood up and ran over to the swing at the other end of the lawn. She didn't just swing. She somehow stood on the swing and held the swing ropes in such a way that her body was suspended completely horizontally. I have never seen that before. It was as if her joy defied gravity. The energy flowed through her system in a way that it just ignored the gravitational obstacles. She was free. She moved through the grass like a leopard, on all fours, but smoothly, majestically, intentionally. She swung her long arms forward and backward, smiling, laughing, doing a sun dance, a gratefulness, happiness, freedom ritual. Her face and her whole body were completely open, in total harmony with everything around her. I stared at her in awe. "This is what happiness is," I thought to myself. No reservation. No condition. No particular reason. No interpretation. No past. No future. I remembered the words of Malidoma, the divination shaman: "You [Lina and me] you are going to be like sisters." This was now true. The next morning, as Lina was still sleeping and I was making my morning coffee in the kitchen downstairs, I looked out the window. Two giant hawks, larger than I have ever seen, sat on the fence out in the field where Lina had been dancing. They flew up to the tree at the end of the field. Playing, watching, having fun. Beautiful, graceful, powerful, deeply present.

There is no one to cure. Nothing to fix. Everything just is.

Winter has passed.

Lina and I are sitting on the couch. She is looking at pictures on my phone. I am staring at her, as usual, wondering what's going on in that mystical mind of hers. I put my glasses on and pick up *The Essential Rumi* by Coleman Barks.

"Rumi is less interested in language," I read aloud from the introduction to the 3rd Chapter on Emptiness and Silence, "and more attuned to the sources of it."

I want to give Lina a well-rounded education, providing her with ideas from many different directions, helping her feel less like an awkward autism outsider and more like who she is—someone with a truckload of seemingly impossible challenges that aren't evaporating anytime soon, yes, definitely. But also, a deeply spiritual being and with an intelligent mind, someone who can grasp many different perspectives without effort and regret.

"Language and music are possible only because we're empty, hollow, and separated from the source," I read and look over at Lina, finding her quiet alertness an indication for me to continue quoting my favorite poet.

"All language is a longing for home."

My tall, beautiful daughter is deeply sunk into the couch as she glances through hundreds and hundreds of pictures of our life together, most of them versions of us, me and her and Elsa, on various hikes, through rain, snow, and hot summer days, across wide open fields, through woods, alongside rivers, lakes, and oceans.

"Is that one reason why you don't talk, Lina? Because you don't want to be separated from the source?" I ask, "or is it completely unintentional?"

She keeps browsing nonchalantly through the pictures, taking her time to respond. I wait, sensing the possibility of her delivering something that I will have to think about; something that isn't as obvious and predictable as the conventional talking that goes on between most humans. Over the years, I have learned the signs.

"It is completely wonderful," she says, without taking her eyes off the pictures.

I sit there quietly, thinking about what she just said. Completely wonderful. She must be talking about how completely wonderful it is to not be separated from the source.

"I see," I say, but the truth is I am not sure what I see. I am trying to work myself around some kind of understanding of what she just volunteered, so obvious and simple to her but much less available to me as I have lived and breathed in this earthly existence for fifty-three years now.

"I see," I say again, feeling slow and foggy. "So you're saying, you don't want to lose that, you don't want to risk being separated from the source?"

She doesn't ever answer this kind of penetrating question. I sit there wondering how ethical it would be for me to tell her that maybe she wouldn't have to be separated from the source, maybe she could have her connection with the source as well as a free-flowing verbal language. But I realize that I don't know that. I don't know if she has any kind of choice in the matter or what would happen with her internally if she actually were capable of choosing to be fully verbal and functioning in society the way most of us are. So I just continue staring at her, hoping that next time we do RPM or next time I read her something interesting that relates to her autism and her language and the degree to which she is trapped or protected by her challenges, she will help me understand a little more about who she is, where she is going, and what I can do to ease her journey.